GLOBE

The best of
CAPE TOWN

PETER JOYCE

NEW
HOLLAND

GLOBETROTTER™

First edition published in 2004
by New Holland Publishers (UK) Ltd
London • Cape Town • Sydney • Auckland
10 9 8 7 6 5 4 3 2

website: www.newhollandpublishers.com

Garfield House, 86 Edgware Road
London W2 2EA
United Kingdom

80 McKenzie Street
Cape Town 8001
South Africa

14 Aquatic Drive
Frenchs Forest, NSW 2086
Australia

218 Lake Road
Northcote, Auckland
New Zealand

Distributed in the USA by
The Globe Pequot Press, Connecticut

ISBN 1 84330 616 6

Publishing Manager (UK): Simon Pooley
Publishing Manager (SA): Thea Grobbelaar
DTP Cartographic Manager: Genené Hart

Editor: Nicole Engeler
Designer: Lellyn Creamer
Cover design: Lellyn Creamer, Nicole Engeler
Cartographer: Nicole Engeler
Picture Researcher: Colette Stott
Proofreader: Melany McCallum

Reproduction by Hirt & Carter (Pty) Ltd, Cape Town
Printed and bound by Times Offset (M) Sdn. Bhd.,
Malaysia.

Photographic Credits:
Shaen Adey: pages 36, 83; Africana Museum:
page 9; Captour: page 8; Gerald Cubitt: pages
11, 29, 30, 41, 48, 50, 63, 84; Roger de la
Harpe: pages 26, 44; Walter Knirr: front cover
page 28; Anne Laing: page 13; Alain Proust:
pages 34, 42; Peter Ribton: page 15; Mark
Skinner: pages 33, 46; SIL: pages 24, 25, 60,
61; SIL/Shaen Adey: pages 18, 23, 49, 70, 73;
SIL/Leonard Hoffman: pages 7, 19, 47; SIL/
Simon Lewis: page 40; SIL/ Peter Pickford:
page 72; SIL/Janek Szymanowski: page 35;
SIL/Erhardt Thiel: title page, pages 6, 10, 12,
16, 20, 21, 22, 27, 31, 37, 39, 45, 52, 53, 54,
57, 62, 66, 74, 76, 77, 78, 80; Stans and
Downing: page 71; Touchline Photo/Tertius
Pickard: page 43; V & A Waterfront
Company: page 65; Mark van Aardt: pages
14, 17, 79; Keith Young: pages 32, 81, 82.
[SIL: Struik Image Library]

Front Cover: *The view of Table Mountain from
Blouberg is arguably one of the most famous
sights in the world.*
Title Page: *The rugged east face of Table
Mountain massif frames the delicate beauty
of Kirstenbosch.*

CONTENTS

MAKE THE MOST OF YOUR GUIDE

Reading these two pages will help you to get the most out of your guide and save you time when using it. Sites discussed in the text are cross-referenced with the cover maps – for example, the reference 'Map B–C3' refers to the Cape Town Map (Map B), column C, row 3. Use the Map Plan below to quickly locate the map you need.

MAP PLAN

Outside Back Cover   Outside Front Cover

Inside Front Cover   Inside Back Cover

THE BIGGER PICTURE

Key to Map Plan

A – Excursions
B – Cape Town
C – Cape Peninsula
D – V & A Waterfront
E – Kirstenbosch National
     Botanical Garden
F – Paarl
G – Stellenbosch
H – Franschhoek
I – Cape Town
     International Airport

Key to Symbols

⊠ — address
☎ — telephone
📠 — fax
🖥 — website
✇ — e-mail address
🕘 — opening times
🚌 — tour
💰 — entry fee
🍽 — restaurants nearby

Map Legend

motorway	▬▬▬	main road	**Adderley**
national road	▬▬▬	other road	Corporation
main road	▬▬▬	mall	ST GEORGE'S MALL
mountain pass	▬▬▬	built-up area	▢
railway	───────	one-way arrow	←
river	〰	viewpoint	⋇
route number	N1	golf course	⌐
city	CAPE TOWN	parking area	P
major town	⊙ Paarl	building of interest	Houses of Parliament
town	O Hout Bay	library	📖
large village	◎ Langebaan	post office	⊠
village	O Pringle Bay	tourist information	i
airport	✈	place of worship	△
place of interest	● Mariner's Wharf	police station	●
mountain peak	Signal Hill ▲ 350 m	bus terminus	🚌
hotel	Ⓗ CAPE SWISS	hospital	⊕
park & garden	Company's Gardens		

Keep us Current

Travel information is apt to change, which is why we regularly update our guides. We'd be most grateful to receive feedback from you if you've noted something we should include in our updates. If you have any new information, please share it with us by writing to the Publishing Manager, Globetrotter, at the office nearest to you (addresses on the imprint page of this guide). The most significant contribution to each new edition will be rewarded with a free copy of the updated guide.

Above: *The beach at Strandfontein is backed by the sandy plain known as the Cape Flats.*

CAPE TOWN

South Africa's '**Mother City**', located at the southern tip of the continent, enjoys a matchless setting. Nestling snugly in the natural amphitheatre formed by the immensity of **Table Mountain** and the blue waters of **Table Bay**, it is a modern, cosmopolitan, stylishly attractive metropolis of graceful thoroughfares, handsome buildings and glittering shops – and it is fast becoming one of the southern hemisphere's premier tourist destinations.

The city proper occupies the northern part of the **Cape Peninsula** – a scenic finger of land, 54km (34 miles) long – that ends, dramatically, in the towering headland known as Cape Point.

Powerful attractions of the city include a near-perfect Mediterranean climate, landscapes that delight the eye, spectacular beaches, the grandeur of Table Mountain, the exuberant Waterfront development, fine hotels, a myriad eating and drinking places, a lively and entertaining calendar of arts, and an enchanting wineland-and-mountain hinterland.

The Land
Climate

Cape Town falls within the winter-rainfall belt, its climate **Mediterranean** in character. Weather patterns are complex and conditions variable, but generally the summers are hot, sunny and very dry. The heat can be oppressive, especially when the warm 'berg wind' blows in from the interior. More often the air is cooled by a gusty, unnerving and sometimes violent (or 'black') southeaster that may reach gale force and last for a week or even longer. The wind is commonly known as the *Cape Doctor* for its supposedly cleansing effect on the city.

Winter is known as the green season. The moist, prevailing wind from the northwest brings damp chill and driving rain, and snow to the mountains of the coastal rampart. The long, cold, wet spells, though, are invariably broken by brief and delightfully unexpected intervals of warmth and welcome sunshine.

Plant Life

The region's natural heritage is both unique and fascinating. Indigenous vegetation largely comprises the *fynbos* ('fine bush') of the **Cape Floral Kingdom**, a zone which extends over the southern coastal belt and contains about 8500 different species. Of these, some 2600 are found on the Peninsula itself.

Most of the plants are low-growing and hardy, well adapted to withstand the summertime droughts. Some are quite lovely; the more prominent include the **proteas**, more than 600 different kinds of **erica** (heath), the reed-like restios, the lilies, orchids, red-hot pokers and disas.

Around 80% of the different plant types are confined to particular areas of the Kingdom, some even to micro-habitats of a few square metres, which renders them especially vulnerable to human encroachment. It has been reckoned that more than 1500 species are threatened with extinction.

Proteas of the Cape
The Western Cape is home to most of South Africa's 368 species of protea (indeed they are named after Proteus, a mythological Greek god who could change his shape at will). Among the best-known proteas are the **sugarbush** (*Protea repens*), the **waboom** or wagon-tree (*Protea nitida*), which grows to 7m (23ft), and the **king protea** (*Protea cynaroides*), which has the largest and most attractive flowers of all the species and is South Africa's national flower.

Below: *The king protea, a fine example of Cape fynbos.*

The Earliest Explorers

The 15th-century **Portuguese** navigators were not the first to see Africa's southernmost shores. Two centuries earlier, **Phoenician galleys** rounded the Cape, although unlike later voyagers they sailed down the east coast. They had been sent by the pharaoh, Necho, to sail past Zanzibar and return 'through the Pillars of Hercules' (Gibraltar). According to Greek historian Herodotus, the Phoenicians reported that, in sailing around Libya (the ancient name for Africa), they 'had the sun on their right hand'. So, they had travelled westwards past Cape Point!

Below: *A rare plate bearing the monogram of the Dutch East India Company.*

History in Brief

Cape Town was born on 6 April 1652 when Commander **Jan van Riebeeck** led his small party of Dutch settlers ashore to establish a replenishment station for the Indies-bound trading fleets of the Dutch East India Company's great maritime empire.

Jan van Riebeeck's instructions were to cultivate friendly relations with the local inhabitants – **Khoikhoi** (Hottentots), semi-nomadic, cattle-owning people related to the San (Bushmen). The colonists needed fresh meat, the Khoikhoi were keen to barter, and for the most part the two cultures managed to coexist in reasonable harmony. Later, rivalry for grazing land and trading rights was to lead to open conflict.

The Early Years

Within days of landing, Van Riebeeck had marked out the site of a **fort**, and before the end of April the first walls were up and supporting five cannons. In due course it was to be replaced by a splendid, new five-sided bastion known as **The Castle**, today South Africa's oldest occupied building.

During the first few years, other basics of civic life made their appearance: a hospital, jetty, simple houses and a scattering of public buildings. Linking the shoreline with the Company's garden was the elegant, oak-lined, stone-paved **Heerengracht**, which was renamed **Adderley Street** during the late 19th century. By the time that the British displaced the Dutch at the end of the 18th century, Cape Town had grown into an elegant little place, one of the southern hemisphere's busiest ports and host to ships and sailors from a dozen nations.

Above: *Charming Adderley Street in the 1830s.*

The British Occupation

With the decline of the Netherlands towards the end of the 18th century, the British first took control of the Cape in 1795, and some time later withdrew from the colony for about eight years. They returned, however, in 1806 and the territory became a **Crown Colony** in 1814, progressing first to representative government (1854) and finally to full self-government (1872) with a constitution modelled on the two-chamber Westminster system. The vote was based on income and property rather than on race – this was a concession to democracy that the apartheid politicians later withdrew. A high commissioner was appointed to look after British interests and, with **Union** in 1910, the colony became one of the country's four provinces, with Cape Town designated the nation's legislative capital.

Growing Up

Around the middle of the 1800s Cape Town's population stood at a modest 24,000, but the latter half of the century brought rapid growth, fuelled by revenue from the fabulous Kimberley diamond fields far to the north and from the city's ever-busier harbour.

Men of Men

When the Dutch colonists arrived, the Cape was occupied by an estimated 6000 **Khoikhoi**, a name that translates as 'men of men'. The Peninsula Khoikhoi (Hottentots) were divided into two main groups, seminomadic clans who kept cattle, lived in simple reed huts, fashioned metal jewellery and cultivated tobacco. The Dutch were soon bartering goods with them, exchanging copper, brass, iron, beads, knives, salt and alcohol for much-needed fresh meat and livestock.

Above: *The harbour is among the southern hemisphere's biggest.*

The Cruel Sea
Over the centuries more than 1300 ships have been wrecked along South Africa's rocky coasts. In the great gale of 1865 no fewer than 11 vessels sank in Table Bay alone. Numerous others foundered on or close to the coasts. Among the many sea-related tales is that of **Wolraad Woltemade**, who braved the ocean seven times to rescue survivors from *De Jonge Thomas*, wrecked in the bay in June 1773. On the eighth trip, both he and his horse disappeared beneath the waves.

The first tarred road was laid in the 1850s (timber paving had previously been tried, but it proved too slippery), as was the inaugural railway line – between **Adderley Street** and the Winelands' town of **Wellington**. The original locomotive built in Scotland in 1859 and shipped out for assembly, is on view in the main station concourse. Horse-drawn trams were introduced in 1863, initially operating between the city and the ocean suburb of **Sea Point**. The first motor car took to the streets in 1895, and a year later the electric tram heralded the demise of the horse as Cape Town's principal means of transport.

By the end of the century the central area had developed beyond recognition and Cape Town had acquired its own unique character as the 'gateway to Africa'. Ships' chandlers did a roaring trade, **Union Castle** mailships regularly offloaded cargoes of immigrants, seamen from a score of far-flung lands haunted the taverns and lodging houses, and attractive hotels catered for the more well-to-do visitors.

Cape Town Today

For centuries Cape Town was known as the **Tavern of the Seas**, drawing much of its prosperity from its harbour. Maritime traffic has declined over the past few decades and the harbour, second in size only to Durban's, is very much quieter than it was in the heydays of the great East Indiamen sailing ships and, later, the passenger steamers.

Still, Cape Town remains a major port city. **Ship repair** is a thriving industry; the dry-dock here is the southern hemisphere's largest; mercantile enterprises contribute a lot to a local economy that also embraces marine fisheries, petroleum refining, light (and increasingly high-tech) engineering, manufacturing (most notably clothing and textiles), banking, insurance and other services – and, of course, **tourism** is a rapidly expanding industry.

The metropolitan area, recently consolidated within what is known as the 'unicity', extends southwards, along the suburban railway line, through Observatory, Mowbray, Rondebosch, Newlands and Wynberg to the historic naval centre of Simon's Town, near Cape Point. The fashionable western or 'Atlantic' suburbs are closer to the city. The northern and eastern (Cape Flats) areas are dense with industrial and residential development that includes Bellville, which gained city status in the 1970s, the relatively new town of Mitchell's Plain, the townships of Langa, Nyanga, Gugulethu and Khayelitsha, and a number of massive, ultra-modern mall complexes.

The People

Greater Cape Town's population totals well over three million, a figure that will rise by another million and more within the next decade if the present pattern of 'urban drift' continues. The largest of the population 'groups' in the city is the mixed-descent or

The First Vintage

The Western Cape's flourishing **wine industry** has its origins in the very first year of white settlement. Just a month after stepping ashore in April 1652, **Jan van Riebeeck** asked his masters in Amsterdam for 'vines which ought to thrive as well on these hill slopes as they do in Spain and France'. In due course 12,000 were growing on his private farm, and in 1659 he was able to confide to his journal that 'today, praise be to God, wine can be made for the first time from Cape grapes, namely from the new must fresh from the vat'. Well before the end of the century grapes were being harvested around **Stellenbosch**, **Franchhoek** and **Paarl**.

Below: *Harvesting Cape wines, which have gained worldwide recognition.*

Music of the Streets
The **Cape Coloured** community has a lively musical tradition, drawn from a rich cultural heritage. Although the origins of many of the *ghomma*-style songs are obscure, the cheerful and sometimes racy words and melodies are still heard at gatherings. The **Minstrel Carnival** is a wonderfully animated New Year street festival of music and dance that owes much to the early African-American minstrel troupes. On this annual occasion, brightly costumed bands mass together on the **Grand Parade** before making their way along the city's thoroughfares to **Green Point**.

Below: *The colourful Minstrel Carnival enlivens the city's streets each New Year.*

Coloured, a society with diverse roots. It is largely Afrikaans-speaking (though most of its members are fluent in English, spoken with a lilting accent), mainly Christian and wholly Westernized in lifestyle and custom. It does, however, have a distinctive and joyous musical tradition. On New Year's Day, sections of the community put on the **Minstrel Carnival**, an exuberant and marvellously colourful parade through the city's streets.

The Coloured people were a more-or-less integrated part of Cape society until the 1950s when, after some cynical tampering with the constitution, the government removed their voting rights. A decade later many also lost their homes: the renowned **District Six** inner suburb was demolished and its residents moved to the bleakness of the Cape Flats (*see panel, page 31*).

A prominent subgroup are the 200,000 **Cape Muslims**, whose forefathers came, as slaves, from the Indonesian islands and other eastern regions. They were valued for their skills as craftsmen (and for their wonderful cuisine; *see page 61*). Many who were not originally of the faith converted to Islam on arrival.

With the abolition of slavery in the 1830s, a fair number of these highly respected people settled in the picturesque **Bo-Kaap**, also known as the Malay Quarter, (*see page 31*) on the city's western perimeter. There was little intermarriage with other groups, and it has remained a highly ntegrated, devout community. Its members attend their city mosques, and many make pilgrimages, not only to Mecca (as is required of all Muslims who can afford to make the journey) but also to

Above: *Happy faces sporting the South African flag.*

the local *kramats*, or tombs of the holy men.

The majority of Cape Town's Black citizens are migrants or the descendants of migrants from the historic **Xhosa** 'homelands' of the Eastern Cape. Most live on the **Cape Flats**, in the sprawling suburbs of Langa, Nyanga, Gugulethu and Khayelitsha and the surrounding informal settlements; many in appalling conditions.

The Black people of the region have inherited a harsh legacy. Under the apartheid regime the southwestern Cape was deemed a 'Coloured preference area', and if you were a black person you could not get a job or a place to live, and you faced repatriation.

Forced removals did not halt the influx. Poor people continued to pour in from a countryside that could no longer meet their minimum needs. And because they were 'illegal', very little provision was made for them in the way of houses, schools, clinics, roads and services.

South Africa is now a democratic country, movement is no longer restricted, and a lot of money is being invested in upliftment. But huge backlogs remain in the Cape and elsewhere, and these issues definitely pose the greatest challenge of the future.

The Sword Dance
Among the more dramatic of **Cape Muslim** traditions is the *Ratiep*, a sword dance, led by a 'master of ceremonies' (*Khalifa*). It was performed under a self-induced trance during which young men pierced their flesh with swords and other sharp instruments. Remarkably, this did not draw blood and left no wound. Today the ritual has lost its religious relevance and many of the *imams* (spiritual leaders), frown on the practice, though it still takes place as an occasional spectacle.

Above: *The cable station at the top of Table Mountain.*

Table Mountain Cableway
🕐 08:00–22:00 Dec–Apr, 08:30–18:00 May–Nov
✉ Tafelberg Road
☎ (021) 424 0015
📠 (021) 424 3792
🖥 www.tablemountain.net
💰 adults: R105 (return), R55 (single); children (under 17) and SA seniors (over 60): R55 (return), R28 (single); students with valid student cards: R77 (return), R39 (single); toddlers (under 4): free
🍽 Restaurant at the top of the mountain, and one near the lower cable station.

🌀 *See Map C–C2*   ★★★

TABLE MOUNTAIN

The great flat-topped sandstone massif towers 1087m (3566ft) above the city and measures nearly 3km (2 miles) from end to end. From the summit there are spectacular views of central Cape Town, its harbour and Waterfront below, Devil's Peak and Lion's Head to either side, the Hottentot Holland mountains in the east and Cape Point far to the south.

The heights are often obscured by what is known as the 'table cloth': dense clouds that billow across the rim of the mountain to tumble down the northern precipice in a continuous cascade.

Most visitors ride up in the new **gondolas** which replaced the old cable cars when the Table Mountain Aerial Cableway Company upgraded its facilities in 1997. The Swiss manufactured cars, boasting revolving floors and a magnificent 360° view over the city and beyond, carry up to 65 individuals at a time. The service is only suspended if winds exceed 80 kph (48 mph).

Also worth exploring are the imposing formations that stand to either side of Table Mountain. To the west you'll see the sugarloaf shape of **Lion's Head** and its attendant ridge, which ends in the 'rump' of **Signal Hill**, the whole vaguely resembling a lion couchant. Each day the noon gun is fired from its emplacement on Signal Hill. The hill's name derives not from the gun, but from an earlier semaphore station that used to communicate with ships at sea. **Devil's Peak** is notable for two British blockhouses built on its steep slopes.

See Map D | ★ ★ ★

V & A WATERFRONT

The Waterfront is for relaxation rather than for sightseeing. But a fair amount that is of historical interest will emerge as you stroll the precincts.

Take note of the **Time Ball Tower**, once used by passing ships to set their clocks, and the **Old Port Captain's building** (the Waterfront's headquarters). Across the Cut is the **Old Clock Tower**. **Cape fur seals**, oblivious of the passing parade, sun themselves around Victoria basin.

Next to the information centre is **Vaughn Johnson's Wine Shop**, and further along, Mitchell's Brewery, which produces superb draught ale. The Union Castle Building houses the **Telkom Exploratorium** on the first floor, and provides fascinating insights into the digital revolution.

The principal shopping centre here is the **Victoria Wharf** mall: a complex of converted warehouses crammed with upmarket outlets ranging from a biltong bar (biltong is dried raw meat, and a well-loved South African delicacy) through jewellery, clothing and accessories boutiques, to imaginative craft shops. The **King's Warehouse** next door houses a cornucopia of produce and fine food stores.

For people of all ages the Waterfront is an Aladdin's Cave of delights. Open-air entertainment, mime-shows and a mime workshop, a gemstone scratch-patch and boat rides are among the drawcards.

V & A Waterfront
🕐 daily
☎ (021) 408 7600
📠 (021) 408 7605
🖥 www. waterfront.co.za
🍽 Restaurants ranging from traditional Cape fare through Cajun, Italian and Mexican.
🚌 There is a regular bus service between the city centre and the Waterfront.

Telkom Exploratorium
✉ Union Castle Building
🖥 www. exploratorium.co.za
📧 info@ exploratorium.co.za

Below: *The imaginatively conceived Waterfront area.*

Highlights

Cheeky Chums
The lively little **grey squirrels** that delight visitors to the Company's Garden are indigenous to North America. They were introduced to Cape Town in the 1890s by Cape premier Cecil Rhodes, and bred so freely that they soon became familiar residents of forests, parks and suburban gardens throughout the region. They live mainly on pine seeds, nuts, acorns and fruits, but they will also rob birds' nests of eggs. They are very tame.

Below: *The Company's Garden, with cloud-capped Table Mountain in the background. The garden started out, in 1652, as a vegetable patch.*

See Map B–F4	★ ★ ★

THE GARDENS AREA

This is one of the most beautiful of Africa urban parks, a spacious expanse of man cured lawns, fountains and pools, statel oak trees, colourful shrubs and wandering pathways. **Government Avenue** runs along the eastern edge and is a favourite haunt o Capetonian strollers and cheeky squirrels.

Imposing edifices flank the gardens o three sides. Along the east are the **House of Parliament**, the **Tuynhuys**, the **Nationa Art Gallery**, the **Cultural History Museum** and **Bertram House**, an elegant Georgian period museum. Then there's the Grea Synagogue and its neighbour the Ol Synagogue, which houses the treasures o the Jewish Museum.

The **South African Museum** and the adjoining **Planetarium** run along the south western side of the garden.

The northern perimeter is graced b the **South African Library**, which is a majo reference institution containing many ex amples of Africana as well as other rare and priceless books.

THE GARDENS & CASTLE OF GOOD HOPE

See Map B–G4   ★ ★ ★

THE CASTLE OF GOOD HOPE

The massive, five-sided, stone-walled fort, completed in 1679, was originally designed to guard the fledgling Dutch colony from sea invasion but later served as the military, administrative and social hub of the colony.

The Castle has an imposing entrance, embellished with a clock tower, the crest of the United Netherlands, the Dutch East India Company's monogram ('VOC') and the coats of arms of the Company's six chambers in Holland. The tower's bell, cast in 1697, is still rung on occasion. Bisecting the spacious courtyard is a defensive cross-wall known as 'De Kat', which later became notable for a gracefully balustraded rococo balcony (Klein Kat) that looks down on the one-time governor's residence and the grand reception hall.

On display in the Governor's residence are period furnishings, *objets d'art*, ceramics and paintings of the William Fehr collection. The original moat and wooden bridge have been restored. Other renovations and additions include a military museum, the historic Dolphin Pool, two dungeons and the Granary that contains several artefacts unearthed during restoration work.

Above: *Much of the Castle, including its historic moat, has been carefully restored.*

The Castle
🕐 09:00–16:00 daily.
✉ Darling Street
☎/📠 (021) 787 1249
💻 www.castleofgoodhope.co.za
📧 casteel@cis.co.za
💰 adults: R18, children over 5 and students: R8, pensioners: R15.
🍽 De Goewerneur

Mariner's Wharf
🕘 09:00–17:00 (shop),
09:00 until late
(restaurant)
✉ Hout Bay Harbour
☎ (021) 790 1100
📠 (021) 790 7777
🖥 www.
marinerswharf.com
📧 marketing@
marinerswharf.co.za
🍴 Seafood is the
speciality here.

Hout Bay Museum
✉ Andrews Road,
Hout Bay
☎ (021) 790 3270

See Map C–B2   ★ ★ ★

HOUT BAY

Hout Bay's picturesque, small harbour is the headquarters of the Peninsula's crayfish (rock lobster) fleet; other catches include snoek, which is sold on the quay in June and July. The annual **Snoek Festival** occupies a lively weekend during this period.

Busy throughout the year is **Mariner's Wharf**, a complex modelled on its namesake in San Francisco and embracing a seafood bistro, restaurant, fresh fish and live lobster market (also on sale are closed oysters; any pearls you find are yours to keep), nautical gift and curio shops. Across the road is Dirty Dick's and The Big Blue, a lively tavern complex with fine views over the harbour. Battered working boats and squeaky-clean leisure craft rub shoulders along the moorings.

Several boat companies takes sightseers on sunset 'champagne' cruises to Cape Town's Waterfront, and on shorter trips to nearby **Duiker Island**, where in summertime a myriad seabirds – most of them fairly rare Bank cormorants – can be seen and more than 4000 Cape fur seals bask on the rocky shores. Deep-sea game fishing is also on offer.

Other popular attractions here include the **World of Birds** (see page 45) and the **Hout Bay Museum**.

Below: *A scenic view of the Hout Bay harbour with its fishing trawlers.*

See Map C–C6 | ★ ★ ★

CAPE POINT

Cape of Good Hope Nature Reserve's chief drawcard is the spectacular headland at the tip of the Peninsula. Cape Point's cliffs fall sheer for about 300m (985ft) to the ocean, in whose often turbulent waters you can glimpse shoals of **tuna** and **snoek**, sporting **dolphins** and **seals** and, occasionally, the massive bulk of a **southern right whale**. **Albatross, petrel, gannet** and **gull** wheel and cry in the air around the promontory.

Breathtaking vistas unfold from the base of the old lighthouse at the top: from here your eye takes in the far ocean horizons and the sweep of **False Bay** to **Danger Point**, 80km (50 miles) to the east.

Cape Point has its place in seafaring myth. It is off this headland that the *Flying Dutchman*, a phantom sailing ship, has periodically been sighted. Legend has it that a 17th-century Dutch captain, Hendrik van der Decken, his craft crippled by the southern gales, vowed to round the 'Cape of Storms' even if it took him until the Day of Judgement to achieve.

Above: *Looking down to the beach from Cape Point.*

Beware the Baboons
The chacma baboons of the **Cape of Good Hope Nature Reserve** are thought to be the only primates in the world (apart from fish-eating man) that live, largely, off the fruits of the sea, which they garner from the rock pools and beaches at low tide. The baboons are partial to human handouts but in your own interest, and in theirs, keep your vehicle locked and do not feed them.

See Map C–C4

★ ★ ★

SIMON'S TOWN

This substantial and handsome bayside centre is steeped in naval history: it was founded by and named after the energetic Cape governor, Simon van der Stel, in 1687. It's still very much a naval town but not exclusively so. Leisure and commercial craft now crowd the harbour and souvenir and craft shops abound. The local beaches, such as **Seaforth** and **Foxy** beach, are very enticing with their secluded stretches of sand, and **Boulders** beach is famous for its colony of endangered jackass penguins.

The splendid **Old Residency** (now housing the Simon's Town Museum and the tourist information office) was built in 1777 as the governor's out-of-town hideaway. One of the more appealing of the Residency's displays relates to **Just Nuisance**, the beloved Great Dane dog who befriended British sailors during World War II. During his lifetime he was formally ranked as an Able Seaman; on his death he was buried, with full military honours, on a hill overlooking town. A bronze statue of the dog stands in **Jubilee Square**.

In the **South African Naval Museum** there are dioramas of the town and it docks, insights into the realm of coastal defence and much else. Of quite different appeal is the **Warrior Toy Museum**, where you'll find an intriguing display of dolls, lead soldiers, miniature cars and trains.

Simon's Town Museum
🕐 09:00–16:00 Mon–Fri, 10:00–16:00 Sat, 11:00–16:00 Sun and public holidays
✉ Old Residency, Court Road
☎ (021) 786 3046
📠 (021) 786 2391

South African Naval Museum
🕐 10:00–16:00, daily except Good Friday, Christmas, New Year
✉ West Dockyard, Simon's Town
☎ (021) 787 4635
📠 (021) 787 4606
📧 navbro@ telkomsa.net
💰 free

Warrior Toy Museum
🕐 10:00–16:00
✉ St George's Street
☎/📠 (021) 786 1395

⚙ *See Map E* ★ ★ ★

KIRSTENBOSCH

The gardens that sprawl over some 530ha (1310 acres) of Table Mountain's well-watered southern slopes were founded in 1913 to preserve and propagate South Africa's rich floral heritage.

The grounds embrace about half the country's 18,000 species of flowering plant, among them the proteas and ericas of the Cape's unique *fynbos* vegetation: disas, bulbs, succulents, ferns, pelargoniums and the fascintating, primeval cycads.

The greater proportion of this floral wealth can be seen in the relatively small cultivated section. Of special note is the **Cycad Amphitheatre** – a sanctuary for most of southern Africa's 20-odd species of a plant type that first appeared 150 million years ago to reach its ascendancy about 80 million years later, during the last age of the dinosaurs.

The cultivated area is logically arranged in a series of informal spreads that include the **Protea Gardens, Peninsula Garden** and the succulents of the **Mathews Rockery**. For the visually disabled, there's a **Fragrance Garden** and also a **Braille Trail**.

Kirstenbosch is a research centre, and intense study as well as very meticulous documentation are undertaken here in the on-site **Compton Herbarium**.

Kirstenbosch National Botanical Garden
⊙ 08:00–19:00 Sep–Mar and 08:00–18:00 Apr–Aug.
⊠ Rhodes Drive, Newlands
☎ (021) 799 8899
📱 (021) 797 6570
🖥 www.nbi.ac.za
👤 adults R18 entry, students R10, school children (6–18 years old) R5, children under 6 free.
🍴 Kirstenbosch Restaurant
☎ (021) 762 9585
✎ info@kirstenboschrestaurant.co.za

Opposite: *Simon's Town's main street, known as the historical mile.*
Below: *The floral delights of Kirstenbosch.*

⭐ *See* Map C–C2   ★★★

GROOT CONSTANTIA

The lime-washed, gabled and beautifully thatched mansion, perhaps the country's stateliest, was originally conceived and built, and its first vineyards laid out, in 1685 by Cape governor **Simon van der Stel**, who happily spent his declining years there. In 1778 Groot Constantia was bought by the wealthy **Cloete family**, who had an eye for beauty as well as a gift for wine making. In 1791 Hendrik Cloete, the patriarch, added a splendid two-storeyed cellar designed by the French architect Louis Thibault. Its pediment was decorated by sculptor Anton Anreith with a stucco relief of Ganymede, cup-bearer to the Grecian gods, and a bevy of cavorting cherubs. The cellar is now a museum that tells the story of wine and wine-making through the ages.

The main house burned down in 1925, but restoration work over the years has been meticulous, and the place still looks very much as it did at the height of its glory. Inside, you'll find lovely period furniture, tapestries, paintings, exquisite porcelain (Delft, Rhineland, Chinese and Japanese) and *objets d'art*.

Nearby is the **Jonkershuis**, a kind of annexe which, in the early days and among the more affluent Dutch landowners, was reserved for the family's eldest son.

There are tours of the modern cellar, wine tastings and sales for those who would like to invest in a bottle or two, an art gallery and a souvenir shop.

Groot Constantia
Groot Constantia markets about 15 wines and offers tastings and sales.
🕐 Tours held hourly between 10:00 and 17:00 every day of the year except Christmas Day, Good Friday and New Year's Day.
☎ (021) 794 5128
📠 (021) 794 1999
🖥 www.grootconstantia.co.za
💰 adults R8, school children R2, children under 6 free

Restaurants
🍴 Jonkershuis
☎ (021) 794 6255
🍴 The Tavern
☎ (021) 794 1144

Opposite: *Canal Walk at Century City is Africa's biggest shopping centre.*
Below: *Historic Groot Constantia, oldest and stateliest of the Peninsula's homesteads.*

See Map C–D1 ★★★

CENTURY CITY

Century City, in **Milnerton**, is a huge complex of shops, restaurants, offices, residential units and entertainment facilities.

Ratanga Junction is Africa's first full-scale theme park and boasts over 30 exhilarating rides from the 'white-knuckle' thrill ride, *The Cobra* rollercoaster, to more sedate family and children rides. The park, set in 20ha (50 acres) of beautifully landscaped gardens and waterways, operates on a seasonal basis.

With over 400 amazing shops to choose from, **Canal Walk** is Africa's largest and most exciting retail and entertainment centre, offering the most compelling, comparative shopping experience under one roof on the continent. It has been designed to offer more than just an unbeatable shopping experience. From its breathtaking architecture to the live events and promotions staged regularly in its state-of-the-art promotions court, which also beams its own television station to its 40 restaurants, coffee shops and pubs, Canal Walk has been designed to entertain.

Canal Walk
🕑 09:00–21:00 daily
✉ Century City
☎ (021) 555 3600 (visitor's centre), 086 010 1165 (infoline)
📠 (021) 555 3100 (visitor's centre)
🖲 info@ centurycity.co.za
💻 www. centurycity.co.za
🍽 Numerous restaurants and coffee shops.
🚌 shuttle buses from hotels in the city and Atlantic Seaboard.

Ratanga Junction
🕑 Wed–Sun, Nov–May
✉ Sable Road, Century City
☎ 0861 200 300
📠 (021) 550 8556
🖲 info@ratanga.co.za
💻 www.ratanga.co.za
💰 full rider R90, junior rider R39, non rider free
🍽 A variety of themed restaurants.

Above: *The statue of Maria, the wife of founder Jan van Riebeeck.*

See Map B–G3

★★

FORESHORE

This flat, 145ha (358-acre) part of the northern city was reclaimed from the sea in the 1930s and 1940s. Great quantities of sand and silt were dredged up and dumped on the landward side, covering for ever the old harbour, its fine promenade and a beach that was invariably cluttered with rowing boats and oars, tackle boxes, ropes and stone anchors. The area is now bisected by the broad reaches of the **Heerengracht**, notable for its handsome flanking office blocks, its shops, and its central island of lawns, palm trees and fountains. There are statues of Portuguese navigator **Bartolomeu Dias** who rounded the Cape in 1488, founder **Jan van Riebeeck** and his wife **Maria de la Queillerie**, and at the bottom of Adderley Street, the **War Memorial**.

If you walk east along the **Hertzog Boulevard** you'll get to the glass and concrete **Civic Centre** and it's neighbour, **Artscape (Nico Theatre Centre)**, focus of Cape Town's mainstream entertainment.

At the southern end of the Heerengracht (or rather, its Lower Adderley Street extension) sits the busy **railway station**; within its precincts you will find a lively permanent fleamarket.

Cape Town is set for expansion; tourism and the conference trade are especially promising, and the newly completed **Cape Town International Convention Centre** (*see* panel, page 25) is paving the way to growth.

Artscape

The focus of Cape Town's mainstream entertainment is the Artscape (Nico Theatre Centre), on DF Malan Street, Foreshore. The design of the complex is an attractive mix of the grand and the cozy; chandeliers of Italian crystal and Aubusson tapestries grace the spacious foyer of the 1200-capacity Opera House. The main theatre seats 540 people, while the smaller Arena seats an intimate 120.
☎ (021) 410 9800
🖥 www.artscape.co.za

FORESHORE & GROOTE SCHUUR

See Map C–C2 ★★

GROOTE SCHUUR

The original **Groote Schuur Estate**, bequeathed to the nation by 19th-century politician and tycoon Cecil Rhodes and renamed Genadendal by Nelson Mandela, covers the mountain slopes beneath Devil's Peak and extends over parts of Observatory, Mowbray, Rosebank and Rondebosch residential areas. Its most noteworthy component is perhaps the **Groote Schuur** (**'Great Barn'**) **homestead** itself, which began life in the mid-1600s as Jan van Riebeeck's granary and was redesigned in imposing style by turn-of-the-century architect Sir Herbert Baker. It is for occupation by the president, if he so chooses.

The elegant ivy-covered buildings of the **University of Cape Town**'s upper campus hug the hillside overlooking the highway. The university's medical school is housed in nearby **Groote Schuur Hospital** where, in 1967, **Chris Barnard** and his cardiac team performed the world's first successful human heart transplant operation.

By taking the off-ramp just past the university, you will reach the imposing **Rhodes Memorial**, the unashamedly imperialistic 'temple' commemorating the great Cecil John Rhodes (for more information, *see* page 36).

Rhodes Memorial
🕐 08:00–18:00 May–Sep, 07:30–19:00 Oct–Apr

Rhodes Memorial Restaurant
🕐 09:00–17:00 daily
☎ (021) 689 9151
📠 (021) 689 9152

Cape Town International Convention Centre (CTICC)
✉ Convention Square, 1 Lower Long Street
☎ (021) 410 5000
📠 (021) 410 5001

Below: *Rhodes Memorial is a monument to Rhodes, who bequeathed his land to the people of South Africa.*

See Map A–B4 ★★

Robben Island Tours
Only the Robben Island Museum conducts official tours of the island. Bookings may be made through the Robben Island Information and Exhibition Centre;
⏰ 07:30–18:00, daily
☎ (021) 419 1300
📠 (021) 419 1057
✉ info@ robben-island.org.za
Tickets may be bought at the Robben Island Museum and the embarkation point at Jetty 1, from where the Makana departs. The trip takes about an hour; tours may take up to three hours.

ROBBEN ISLAND

About 11.5km (7 miles) north out to sea and clearly visible from the shore is oval-shaped Robben Island ('robben' is Dutch for 'seals'), which until recently served as the infamous maximum security prison where **Nelson Mandela**, South Africa's first truly democractically elected president, served much of his 27-year sentence.

Over the decades Robben Island also served variously as a giant livestock pen, a place for lunatics and paupers, the chronically sick and otherwise unwanted, a leper colony, and as a penal colony.

This living museum supports a tiny village of approximately 1200 inhabitants. Among the notable structures to be found here are the 1800s lighthouse, which still performs with honour; the **Church of the Good Shepherd**, designed by celebrated turn-of-the-century architect Sir Herbert Baker, and the old Residency, once the home of the local commissioners.

The major focal point of the island is the rather sombre **Maximum Security Prison**, a bleak place of tiny cells (including Mandela's). The island bus tour also takes in Robert Sobukwe's prison house, the old lime quarry where the prisoners worked and other historic venues.

Below: *A bird's-eye view of Robben Island. Over the centuries the island was used to confine political prisoners and other undesirables.*

ROBBEN ISLAND & NEWLANDS

See Map C–C2 ★★

NEWLANDS

This sprawling, fashionable suburb, about 6km (4 miles) from the city centre, is noted for its densely treed avenues, its international **cricket** and **rugby** grounds, and its unusually high rainfall – the product of wind patterns and the high mountain backdrop.

For rugby enthusiasts, Newlands is something of a mecca. The recently expanded stadium hosted the opening match of the 1995 World Cup, among the latest of a long sequence of significant contests stretching back to 1891, when WE Maclagen led the first British team onto a South African field. In the decades that followed, South Africa reached and maintained a pre-eminent position in international rugby until its enforced isolation during the wilderness years of apartheid. Much of the story is told by the **South African Rugby Museum**, largest of its kind in the world.

On the banks of the Liesbeeck River close to the stadium is the **Josephine Mill**, built in 1840 and named in honour of the Crown Princess of Sweden, who later became queen. It is now Cape Town's only surviving watermill. There are guided tours and daily milling demonstrations, a restaurant and pleasant tea-garden.

Off the M3 highway, to your right as you drive away from the city , you'll see the tall trees of **Newlands forest**, a delightful place for picnics and barbecues and favoured by brisk walkers, hikers and joggers.

Above: *The sylvan tranquility of Newlands forest.*

South African Rugby Museum
🕐 08:30–17:00
Mon–Fri
✉ Boundary Road, Newlands
☎/📠 (021) 686 2151
🛇 Admission charged.

Josephine Mill
🕐 09:00–16:00 weekdays. Sunday concerts are held outdoors at the mill in summer (Nov–Feb), usually starting at 17:30.
✉ Boundary Road, Newlands
☎/📠 (021) 686 4939
🍽 Miller's Plate Restaurant:
☎ (021) 685 6233

Below: *The family beach at Fish Hoek, a False Bay town.*

| ⊙ *See* Map C–C4 | ★ ★ |

FISH HOEK

The Rising Land

Not too long ago on the geophysical calendar the 'waist' of the **Peninsula** – the low-lying plain running across its width between Fish Hoek and Noordhoek – lay beneath the sea. Over the course of 20,000 icy years the sea level dropped a dramatic 120m (nearly 400ft) and then, as the climate warmed, rose again – but not to its original height. The Peninsula thus assumed its present character little more than 10,000 years ago.

A solidly respectable seaside town (until quite recently it was one of the only 'dry' municipalities in South Africa: no alcohol could be sold within its boundaries), Fish Hoek is noted chiefly for its fine family beach and the warm summertime offshore waters bright with yachts, sailboards and catamarans. The gentle **Jager Walk**, along the shoreline rocks, fills a pleasant hour, and the rock pools are very popular with young children.

High above the valley that forms the 'waist' of the Cape Peninsula is the celebrated **Peers Cave**, an important archaeological site and, approximately 15,000 years ago, home to **Fish Hoek Man**. The walls of the cave are decorated with prehistoric paintings and there are lovely views of the Peninsula from the summit.

FISH HOEK & KALK BAY

See Map C–C3   ★★

KALK BAY

This is an enchanting little harbour and resort village further up the coast from Fish Hoek. 'Kalk' is the Afrikaans word for 'lime', and the bay was so named because all the shells collected along the coast were burnt there in order to provide whitewash and mortar for the colonial buildings.

Today the main commercial activity in Kalk Bay is **fishing**; catches are sold on the quayside; the place is especially lively during June and July, when the snoek are running. Along the Main Road and alleys in the village are antique, pottery and junk shops, art galleries and restaurants.

Just behind the coastline, between the village and Muizenberg, are the **Kalk Bay mountains**, a modest but scenically striking range of hills cut through by a labyrinth of underground chambers. Many have odd-ball names (such as Mirth Parlour, Dolly's Doorway, Light and Gloom, Creepy Corridor), and they're worth exploring, though it's suggested you do so with someone who knows their way around. This untamed and rocky area is also a drawcard for hikers, ramblers, bird-spotters and lovers of nature.

Fresh Fish for Sale
At around noon each day Kalk Bay's little fishing boats return to harbour laden with the fruits of the sea, which are then auctioned off in lively and good-humoured fashion from the quayside. The prices are attractively low, and you can have your fish cleaned on the spot, fresh and ready to take home for the traditional South African 'braai' (barbecue).

Below: *The pretty little village and harbour of Kalk Bay.*

See Map B–F4 | ★

Golden Acre
✉ Corner Adderley
and Strand Streets
🕘 Shops generally
open 08:30–17:00
Mon–Fri, 8:30–13:00
Sat, closed Sun.

Opposite: *A Muslim
couple, with two
of the area's flat-
roofed houses in
the background.*
Below: *Adderley
Street is Cape
Town's busiest
thoroughfare.*

ADDERLEY STREET

The striking feature of the city's busiest
street (named after a 19th-century British
politician) is the vast **Golden Acre Centre**,
comprising a cavernous hall and concourses
packed with department stores, speciality
shops, eateries and cinemas. Its many glittering passageways run maze-like beneath
the wider neighbourhood to link (among
much else) the railway station, the coach
terminal, two parking garages and the sky-
scraping five-star Cape Town Holiday Inn.
The Golden Acre is thought to be the site of
the Dutch settlers' first earth-and-timber
fort. A small reservoir, dating back to 1663,
was uncovered during building operations
of the Golden Acre and a portion of it
remains on display.

Just a few paces further up the bustling
Adderley Street are the famous Cape Town
flower-sellers;
these raucous and
good-humoured
street vendors in-
vite bargain and
banter and will
sell you proteas,
carnations, irises,
roses and gladioli
at surprisingly low
prices.

Situated a bit
further up is the
**Dutch Reformed
Groote Kerk**, or
'Great Church' (*see*
page 34).

See Map B–F3 | ★

MALAY QUARTER

Situated along the slopes of Signal Hill to the west of the central area is a dense cluster of dainty little single-storey, flat-roofed houses built during the 18th century for Cape Town's cosmopolitan artisan class. The streets are narrow and steep and many of the buildings are brightly painted. The minarets of mosques rise above the low skyline, and the call of the muezzin charms the evening air.

This is the Malay Quarter, more correctly known as **Bo-Kaap**, and home to several thousand members of the Cape's Islamic society. Many of the residents are descendants of slaves who, after emancipation in the 1830s, moved into the area to form a very close-knit community, bound together by its Indonesian culture and faith.

For the rest, much of the heritage of the Malay Quarter is intact, evident in the religion, in a cuisine that has evolved into a cornucopia of classic Cape dishes, in some of the customs and rituals and, on special occasions, in mode of dress.

A little of this can be seen in the **Bo-Kaap Museum** (see page 38), which is housed in a 1760s period house – Cape Town's oldest surviving town residence.

The Bo-Kaap's restaurants serve Malay food (no alcohol allowed). Do not explore the area on your own; tours can be arranged through Cape Town Tourism.

District Six

East of the city centre is a patch of ground that was once home to 55,000 mostly **Coloured** people. In 1966 District Six was declared a 'white' area and the residents were moved to other townships on the bleak Cape Flats. The suburb was demolished and the area lay fallow for three decades. Now the land is to be returned to about 45,000 original inhabitants and their descendants. The District Six Beneficiary and Redevelopment Trust is monitoring the development of this important landmark.

Right: *Clifton's beaches in high summer. The water tends to be chilly, but the sands are sheltered from the prevailing winds.*

See Map C–B1   ★

Sun, Sea and Sand
The long stretch of the Peninsula's west coast between Sea Point and Camps Bay, known as the '**Cape Riviera**', is especially attractive. Clifton has four fashionable beaches. Also close-by are Maiden's Cove (for skin-diving), Glen Beach (for surfing) and Camps Bay (for sunbathing). Llandudno is scenically beautiful; Sandy Bay is for all-over tanning. The Cape of Good Hope Nature Reserve has several pleasant and safe spots; Maclear beach is excellent for scuba-diving and bathing. Muizenberg on the Peninsula's east coast has a long and beautiful beach. St James has a sheltered, tidal pool and Boulders has safe bathing and a penguin sanctuary.

ATLANTIC SEABOARD

West of the city is **Green Point**, noted for its pleasant Common, golf course and Green Point Lighthouse.

Next-door **Sea Point** is a busy, bustling, cosmopolitan area dense with luxurious apartment and time-share blocks, hotels, restaurants, discos, delis and nightspots. The Main Road is a glitzy, noisy, fun thoroughfare, though the tinsel is a bit tarnished in places. The 3km (2-mile) lawn- and palm-graced promenade is much favoured by Capetonian strollers. At the end of Beach Road is the Sea Point Pavilion.

From Sea Point you drive through **Bantry Bay** to **Clifton**, famed for its four inviting beaches. Further along, **Camps Bay** also boasts a fine expanse of sand, but has more amenities (tidal pool, shops, theatre, restaurants, and an excellent hotel called The Bay), though both centres remain affluent residential areas rather than playgrounds.

See Map C–C3   ★

MUIZENBERG

Cecil Rhodes died in 1902 in his small, plain, thatch-roofed, stone-walled holiday cottage just off the Main Road between St James and Muizenberg. The house has been preserved as a museum; photographs and personal memorabilia recall the life and times of one of colonial South Africa's most controversial figures.

The Fort is an impressive Italianesque building that houses the old masters of the **Natale Labia Museum**; also on view are examples of the modern English painting school and some fine furniture. Further along Main Road is the **South African Police Museum** and **Die Posthuys**. The latter dates back to 1673 and served then as a signal house and small fort.

The town's genteel past is reflected in the Victorian villas, Edwardian boarding houses, renovated cottages and the imposing ediface on the railway station designed by Herbert Baker. The candy-striped pavilion offers swimming, miniature-train rides, boat trips, a waterslide and playground.

The **Silvermine Nature Reserve** extends inland from the Muizenberg area. On the northern side of town is a delightful stretch of water called **Sandvlei**, which is popular among canoeists and watersportsmen. The eye-catching waterfront suburb of **Marina da Gama** flanks the lake's eastern shore.

Seaside Stroll
Attractive features of **St James** are its gaily painted Victorian-type wooden bathing huts, its safe tidal pool, sheltered beach and rock pools bright with marine life. There is a very pleasant 3km (2-mile) walkway leading along the shoreline to Muizenberg. Points of interest en route (along Main Road and reached via a subway) include Rhodes Cottage and the Rust en Vrede mansion, designed by Sir Herbert Baker in the Cape Dutch Revival style. Die Posthuys, which is a whitewashed cottage, and Muizenberg railway station, are proclaimed national monuments.

Below: *Muizenberg is famed for its long, broad white sands and its rather old-fashioned charm.*

Above: *The old Lutheran Church on Strand Street.*

Places of Worship

St George's Anglican Cathedral

Apartheid was often protested from this cathedral. Listen to superb choral music and hear the sermons of Archbishop Njongonkulu Ndungane, successor to Nobel Laureate Desmond Tutu. (Don't miss the lovely rose window.)
✉ *Wale Street, Gardens,*
☎ *(021) 424 7360,*
📠 *(021) 423 8466,*
✆ *vestry@ stgeorgescathedral.com*
💻 *www. stgeorgescathedral.com*

Groote Kerk

The Groote Kerk is the country's oldest formal place of worship. It was consecrated in 1841, but incorporates the steeple of its 1704 predecessor, and is noted for its pulpit, vaulted timber roofing and gravestones that serve as paving slabs.
✉ *Adderley Street,*
☎ *(021) 461 7044,*
📠 *(021) 461 7620.*

Lutheran Church

This church was built in 1771 (and later redesigned) as a kind of warehouse – a necessary disguise since, at that time, any religion other than Dutch Reformed was barely tolerated by officialdom. The entrance, organ-loft and pulpit are the work of sculptor Anton Anreith.
✉ *Strand Street.*

St Mary's Catholic Cathedral

This elegant cathedral is situated opposite Tuynhuys and the Houses of Parliament.
✉ *16 Bouquet Street,*
☎ *(021) 461 1167,*
📠 *(021) 461 9330,*
💻 *www. catholic-ct.org.za*

Jamai Mosque

Cape Town's oldest mosque was built in 1850. It is also known as Queen Victoria Mosque, as it stands on land donated by the British monarch.
✉ *66 Chiappini Street, Malay Quarter.*

Historic Buildings

Houses of Parliament

The Houses of Parliament, built in 1884, are recognized as an architectural masterpiece. The gallery is open to the public during parliamentary sessions (Jan–Jun); tickets are available from Room 12.

✉ Parliament Street,
☎ (021) 403 2911,
🕓 guided tours take place Mon–Fri Jul–Jan.

Tuynhuys

The Colonial Regency style Tuynhuys was once a pleasure lodge and is now the president's city office. Spare a glance for the equestrian statue of General Louis Botha, guerrilla leader during the Anglo-Boer War (1899–1902) and then prime minister from 1910–19, that stands on Stal Plein in front (on the Plein Street side) of Tuynhuys.

✉ Plein Street,
☎ (021) 464 2100,
📠 (021) 464 2217.

Koopmans-De Wet House

A classic example of 18th-century Cape domestic architecture, the house was home to Maria Koopmans-De Wet (1838–1906), a leading socialite, connoisseur, patron of the arts, Afrikaner nationalist and, generally, a formidable political lady who was placed under house arrest for campaigning against the infamous concentration camps of the Anglo-Boer War.

✉ 35 Strand Street,
☎ (021) 481 3935,
🕓 09:30–16:00 Tue–Thu.

The Castle of Good Hope

See page 17 for details.

Pathfinder for Islam
Perhaps the most eminent of the Cape's early **Muslims** was **Sheik Yusuf**, a 17th-century holy man and rebel against the Dutch in the East Indies. Yusuf is regarded as the founder of the region's Islamic community, and his kramat is one of six shrines that together form a 'holy circle'. The kramats – five on or near the Peninsula and one on Robben Island – are carefully maintained, brightly decorated and regularly visited by the devout.

Below: The stately Houses of Parliament opposite the Company's Garden.

City Hall

Nelson Mandela delivered his famous address from the balcony of the City Hall, a grandly ornate granite and marble edifice designed in the Italian Renaissance style and completed in 1905. Its clock tower, modelled on (though just half the size of) London's Big Ben, houses southern Africa's largest carillon of 39 bells. The main hall, where orchestral and choral concerts are frequently held, has a magnificent 3165-pipe organ and is also the venue for the more lavish of civic functions.

⊠ *Grand Parade, Darling Street,*
☎ *(021) 465 2029.*

Rhodes Memorial

This grand and stately neoclassical structure, the work of architect Sir Herbert Baker, incorporates a powerful piece of statuary entitled *Physical Energy* sculpted by FG Watts, together with the four pairs of lion-sphinxes and a bust of Rhodes by JW Swan, beneath which is inscribed Kipling's moving tribute to 'the immense and brooding spirit'.

⊠ *Groote Schuur Estate,*
⏰ *08:00–18:00 May–Sep, 07:30–19:00 Oct–Apr.*

Mostert's Mill

A traditional Dutch windmill, this is one of only two such mills remaining in the Cape. Mostert's Mill, which dates from 1796, has been carefully restored and is once again open to the public.

⊠ *Rhodes Avenue, Mowbray,*
☎ *(021) 762 5127 or 088 129 7168.*

Below: *The turn-of-the-century City Hall, built of ornate granite in Italian Renaissance style.*

Museums and Galleries

South African Cultural History Museum

Exhibits housed within this museum include thematic displays and a wealth of Oriental and other *objets d'art*. The building started life as the slave lodge and was later converted to the Supreme Court. Let your eyes wander up to the rear pediment carved by Anton Anreith: it bears a caricature of the British Lion and Unicorn, rare humour from an otherwise dour Calvinistic past.
✉ *Corner of Adderley and Wale Streets,*
☎ *(021) 460 8240,*
⊕ *08:30–16:30 Mon–Fri, 09:00–13:00 Sat,*
💻 *www.museums.org. za/sachm/osl/*
♂ *R7, children R2.*

Gold of Africa Museum

A fine 18th-century Cape Dutch townhouse has been beautifully restored and now houses the Gold of Africa Museum. On show are glittering golden artifacts from the African continent.
✉ *Martin Melck House, 96 Strand Street,*
☎ *(021) 405 1540,*
📠 *(021) 405 1541,*
⊕ *09:30–17:00,*
♂ *adults R20, scholars and pensioners R16 and pre-schoolers R10.*
💻 *www. goldofafrica.com*

South African National Art Gallery

A repository of some 6500 works of local and European art.
✉ *Government Avenue,*
☎ *(021) 467 4660,*
📠 *(021) 467 4680,*
⊕ *10:00–17:00 Tue–Sun, closed Mon and Workers Day,*
♂ *R5 (Sun free), children free.*

South African Museum

African culture, the huge variety of about 200 million-year-old fossils unearthed from

Above: *The cool, stone-flagged interior of the Old Slave Lodge, part of the South African Cultural History Museum.*

Slavery at the Cape
The first Cape slaves arrived in 1657, from **Angola** and **West Africa**. Later, they were brought in from the Dutch possessions of the **Indies**. Those assigned to work in town were rather better off than their country cousins: they were lodged in the slave quarters and provided with regular meals and schooling for their children. In 1710 there were about 1200 adult slaves in the Dutch colony. By the end of the century, the figure had risen to 17,000 – which was more than the white population of the period. Slavery was finally abolished in 1834 by Act of Parliament.

Exploring the Southern Skies

The **South African Astronomical Observatory** is the national headquarters of a network of sky-probing installations that includes the advanced complex at **Sutherland**, in the clean-aired Great Karoo far to the north. Sutherland is the site of the multi-million dollar, internationally sponsored Southern African Large Telescope (Salt). It is to be the hemisphere's largest astronomical installation, capable of detecting light as faint as a candle flame on the moon and designed to explore black holes and planets around distant stars. The Cape Town arm of the National Observatory sets South African standard time, and also sends the electrical impulse that fires the familiar noon-day gun on Signal Hill.
✉ just off Liesbeeck Parkway, Observatory,
☎ (021) 447 0025,
🚌 Tours conducted on the second Saturday of each month; phone for an appointment.

the strata of the Great Karoo (including dinocephalians, or 'fearful heads'), and the whales of the southern seas are prominent among the subjects displayed in the South African Museum. Birds, fishes, geology, archaeology and the history of printing also feature.
✉ *25 Queen Victoria Street,*
☎ *(021) 481 3800,*
📠 *(021) 481 3993,*
🕐 *10:00–17:00 daily, closed Christmas Day and Good Friday,*
💰 *adults R8, free on Sundays; students, pensioners and children free.*

Planetarium

Part of the museum complex is the Planetarium, whose projectors reproduce the hemisphere's heavens to illuminate the constellations over a 26,000-year (past, present and future) timespan.
☎ *(021) 481 3900,*
💰 *adults R10, students and pensioners R8, adults evenings R12, school children R5, family (2 adults and 2 children) R20; museum and planetarium: adults R15, children under 16 R5.*

Bo-Kaap Museum

This a 1760s period house and Cape Town's oldest surviving town residence that belonged to the religious leader Abu Bakr Effendi. He hailed from Turkey and, among other things, started an Arabic school in town (he also, oddly enough, wrote one of the first books to be published in Afrikaans). The bedroom is fitted out as a traditional bridal suite; furnishings are typical of an 18th-century Muslim home.
✉ *71 Wale Street,*
☎ *(021) 481 3939,*
📠 *(021) 481 3938,*
🕐 *09:30–16:00 Mon-Sat, closed Sun and Eid holidays,*
💰 *adults R5, scholars R2, children under 6 free.*

South African Maritime Museum

A major Waterfront attraction is the South African Maritime Museum, whose floating exhibits include the historic *SAS Somerset*, the world's sole surviving boom defense vessel, and the steam tug *Alwyn Vincent*. Both are moored in front of the Victoria & Alfred Hotel. On view are a shipwright's workshop, a 'discovery cove' for children and displays relating to shipwrecks, Table Bay harbour (past, present and future), the fishing industry, shipping lines and the romantic era of the Union Castle mailships.

⊠ *Dock Road, V & A Waterfront,* ⊕ *10:00–17:00 daily, closed Good Friday and Christmas,* ☎ *(021) 405 2880,* 📠 *(021) 405 2888,* ⌨ *museum@ maritimemuseum. ac.za* 🖥 *www. maritimemuseum. ac.za*

🎟 *(includes a visit to the SAS Somerset) adults R10, scholars R3, family ticket (2 adults with children) R20, children under 6 free.*

Irma Stern Museum

This museum features the works of one of the country's most prolific and controversial artists. Stern gave the first of her many one-woman shows in Berlin in 1919 but on her return to South Africa her rich, sensual canvases were dismissed as 'revolutionary' (and even immoral), and it was not until the 1930s that she began to gain local acceptance. She died in 1966. On display in her Rosebank home, *The Firs*,

A Summer Garden
The gardens of **Kirstenbosch** are attractive all year round but are best in spring (September and October), when the annuals and many proteas are in bloom, and the bird life at its most animated. Jazz and other concerts enliven summer Sunday evenings. Guided tours are offered during the week. The gardens have been recently enhanced by an impressive new Visitor's Centre, incorporating an information office, book-and-souvenir shop, restaurant, and the modern Glass House Conservatory. (*See* panel, page 21 for further details.)

Below: *Proteas feature strongly in Kirstenbosch Gardens.*

The Old Cape Road
Ou Kaapse Weg ('Old Cape Road', or the M64) is a fine scenic drive that cuts through the **Silvermine Nature Reserve**, running southwest from the Westlake area to climb over the Steenberg ('stony mountain') plateau before descending to Fish Hoek Valley and Noordhoek on the west coast. Along the winding way are a myriad indigenous flowers that are at their colourful best in springtime, and splendid views across the southern Peninsula. Among the most eye-catching vistas is that from just below the entrance to the Silvermine Reserve.

Below: *The placid waters of Silvermine Nature Reserve's upland reservoir.*

are some 200 of her paintings, together with sculptures and her fine collection of antiques, *objets d'art* and African artifacts brought back from the Congo (Zaire).

✉ *Cecil Road, Rosebank,*
🕐 *10:00–17:00 Tue–Sat,*
☎ *(021) 685 5686,*
🎫 *adults R7, scholars and pensioners R3.*

Parks and Gardens
Kirstenbosch
See page 21 for details.

Rondevlei Nature Reserve
Well worth a visit is the Rondevlei Nature Reserve, home to 225 different species, most of them waterfowl. Notables include the Caspian terns, the martial eagle and the African fish eagle. A few hippos hide away among the reeds. Hides, look-out towers equipped with telescopes, a waterfront walkway and a very interesting museum feature among the facilities

✉ *Perth Road, Grassy Park,*
🕐 *all hours.*

Silvermine Nature Reserve
This pristine, 2000ha (4942-acre) wilderness extends over the Steenberg hills, and across the narrow waist of the Peninsula, from Kalk Bay and Muizenberg in the east to Noordhoek in the west. The terrain is rugged, an attractive compound of mountain peak, plateau and forested gorge, upland stream, waterfall and, everywhere, an astonishing floral diversity. Bird life is prolific.
🕐 *all hours.*

ACTIVITIES
Sport and Recreation

There are some exquisite **beaches** strung along the Peninsula's shoreline and up the coast towards Bloubergstrand. Those on the western or 'Atlantic' side are sheltered from the prevailing summer wind but the sea is rather cold for comfortable bathing. On the other hand, False Bay in the east tends to be breezy but water temperatures are about 5°C warmer and reach about 23°C (73°F) in summer. Visitors should stick to popular areas – those monitored by life-savers – rather than seek seclusion. You'll find especially attractive stretches of beach at Clifton and next-door Camps Bay, close to town, and at Muizenberg on the east coast. Noordhoek, in the west, is ideal for an early-morning **horseback ride**.

Above: *The white sands of Clifton's popular 4th Beach.*

The rockier coves beckon the **snorkeller** and **scuba-diver**. There are strict limits for rock lobster and abalone catches. **Sea angling** is virtually unrestricted; rock and surf fishermen reel in snoek, steenbras, red roman and *kabeljou* (kob); game-fishing enthusiasts take marlin, swordfish and three species of tunny (tuna). A number of companies offer game-fishing charters. Because the sea is easily accessible from almost anywhere in the Peninsula, good opportunities for **yachting, power-boating, board-sailing, waterskiing, parasailing** and other aquatic sports are limitless. For those people who

> **Horse Riding**
> A popular pastime on the beach or in the winelands (day and overnight trails).
> **Dunes Racing Stables**
> ⊠ Noordhoek
> ☎ (021) 789 1723
> **The Riding Centre**
> ⊠ Hout Bay
> ☎ (021) 790 5286 or 082 346 4336
> **Horse Riders**
> ⊠ Hout Bay
> ☎ (021) 790 1177 or 082 409 9699

> **Royal Cape Yacht Club**
> ⊠ Small Craft Basin, Table Bay Harbour
> ☎ (021) 421 1354
> 🖷 (021) 421 6028
> 🖥 www.rcyc.co.za

prefer more structured **swimming**, public pools are located in Sea Point (seawater), in the city at the top of Long Street (indoor, heated), and in Newlands (an Olympic-sized pool); there are smaller municipal pools in the suburbs.

Cycling is an exhilarating way of exploring the region. The local pedal-power association organizes weekend excursions and fun rides throughout the year. The annual Argus/Pick 'n Pay Cycle Tour, a challenging 105km (65 miles) around the Peninsula, is held in March and attracts about 24,000 entrants. Participants, however, must register well in advance to avoid disappointment.

Golf (see panel, this page) and **bowling** clubs welcome guests; courses and greens are generally of a high standard.

Bird-watching is a popular activity in the Cape. More than 300 species of birds have been identified in the wider Cape Town area, including sugarbirds, paradise fly-catchers, black eagles that ride the high thermals and a variety of aquatic birds. Bird-watchers have a wide choice of venues, such as the Company's Garden (see page 16) and also Kirstenbosch National Botanical Garden (see page 21). To the north of the city is Milnerton lagoon and the Rietvlei Conservation Area – a major waterfowl breeding reserve, home to the Caspian and Arctic tern, the fish eagle and flamingo and a haven for contaminated or injured seabirds, particularly penguins.

Golf Clubs
Western Province Golf Union
☎ (021) 686 1668
✆ (021) 686 1669
✉ wpga@global.co.za

Mowbray Golf Club
☎ (021) 685 3018
✆ (021) 686 6008
✉ mowbray@global.co.za
🖥 www.mowbraygolf.club.co.za

Rondebosch Golf Club
☎ (021) 689 4176
✆ (021) 685 1447
✉ rgc@mweb.co.za

Metropolitan Golf Club
☎ (021) 434 7808
✆ (021) 434 3563

Westlake Golf Club
☎ (021) 788 2020
✆ (021) 788 2530

Royal Cape Golf Club
☎ (021) 761 6551
✆ (021) 797 5246

Rondevlei Nature Reserve, located near the shores of False Bay, is sanctuary for an even more prolific bird life – 225 species in all. There are two lookout towers with telescopes and five hides to facilitate bird-watching (the reserve also has four hippos). Another rewarding spot is the extensive Cape of Good Hope Nature Reserve (*see page 19*), which covers the southern tip of the Cape Peninsula.

Spectator Sports

Major provincial and international **rugby** and **cricket** matches are played at the famed Newlands stadiums, 7km (4.5 miles) from the centre of the city. **Road running** is a popular pastime and quite competitive, the major event being the Two Oceans marathon, held over Easter each year (12,000-plus entrants). **Athletics** and **soccer** also enjoy wide support.

The government is encouraging private sponsors to continue with their plans to invest in new infrastructure for world-class sporting events.

Western Province Rugby Football Union
✉ 11 Boundary Road, Newlands
🖳 www.wprugby.com
🚌 **Gateway to Newlands:**
☎/📠 (021) 686 2151
📧 gatenew@mweb.co.za
🖳 www.newlandstours.co.za

Western Province Cricket Assosciation
✉ Campground Road, Newlands
☎ (021) 657 2003
📠 (021) 657 2020
📧 info@cricket.co.za
🖳 www.wpca.cricket.org

Opposite: *Sea Point promenade is popular among joggers.*
Left: *Cricket fever reaches its peak at Newlands grounds.*

Two Oceans Aquarium
✉ Dock Road,
V & A Waterfront
☎ (021) 418 3823
📠 (021) 418 3952
📧 aquarium@
aquarium.co.za
🖥 www.
aquarium.co.za
🕐 09:30–18:00, daily
💰 adults R50, children
(4–17 years) R20, chil-
dren under 4 years
free, pensioners R38,
undergraduate stu-
dents R38.

**Topstones Mineral
World**
✉ Dido Valley Road,
Simon's Town
☎ (021) 786 2020
📠 (021) 786 2502
📧 topstones@
iafrica.com

Opposite: *A parrot
at World of Birds.*
Below: *The Two
Oceans Aquarium.*

Fun for Children

Children will love a visit to the walk-
through, window-lined tunnels of the
V & A Waterfront's **Two Oceans Aquarium**.
Here, in all their colourful variety, are
sharks, tuna and about 300 other species
that together form a representative cross-
section of the region's marine heritage.
Highlights include above- and below-water
observation of seals and penguins; a 'touch
tide pool' containing starfish, sea urchins
and much else; a kelp forest, open ocean
tank and special displays of rays and jelly-
fish. Fascinating attractions include a complete coastal ecosystem in miniature, with
waterfalls, mountain streams, mudbanks,
sand flats and inter-tidal rock pools, all
stocked with appropriate plant, bird and
marine life.

Just outside Simon's Town is **Topstones
Mineral World**, reputed to be the world's
biggest gemstone tumbling factory. Here
you can watch huge quantities of rough
stone being converted into highly polished
sparklers, which
are then drilled
and fashioned in-
to jewellery and
souvenirs. Chil-
dren especially
are invited to
visit the cave and
fossick in the
scratch patch; a
large heap of
fragments. What
you select you
can keep, for a
small fee.

Children won't want to miss Hout Bay's **World of Birds**, the largest bird park in Africa – and imaginatively conceived. Its 100 or so spacious walk-through aviaries are landscaped to provide habitats natural to about 3000 residents, which represent 450 different species. Visitors wander at will through the enclosures while the birds carry on with their busy routines – feeding, building nests, bathing, socializing – oblivious of the human presence. In and around

the willow-shaded ponds are freer birds, including cormorants, herons, egrets and swans. There are also endearing monkeys and meercats.

Some 30km (19 miles) from central Cape Town is the **West Coast Ostrich Ranch**. Here visitors can get a closer look at these big birds, purchase souvenirs and taste some ostrich dishes in the restaurant.

GrandWest casino and entertainment world has much to offer children, including an **ice-rink**, six cinemas and an indoor theme park.

Ratanga Junction theme park is a must for children (*see* page 23). Popular rides include the Diamond Devil Run, a 'runaway mine train' rollercoaster, Crocodile Gorge, a rapid river ride, and Bushwacker – a family rollercoaster through the jungle. There are also snake shows and bird shows to enthrall the young ones.

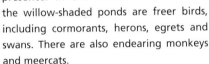

World of Birds
⊠ Sanctuary Valley Road, Hout Bay
☎ (021) 790 2730
📠 (021) 790 4839
📧 worldofbirds@ mweb.co.za
🖥 www. worldofbirds.org.za

West Coast Ostrich Ranch
⊠ Van Schoorsdrif Road, Philadelphia
☎ (021) 972 1669
📠 (021) 972 1905
📧 wkor@iafrica.com
🖥 www. wcor-av.co.za
⏰ 09:00–17:00 daily, tours every half hour

Cape Town Ice Rink
⊠ GrandWest
☎ (021) 535 2260
📠 (021) 535 2263
🖥 www.icerink.co.za

Above: *The stately Old Town House on Greenmarket Square.*

Exploring on Foot
Visitors are free to walk where they wish in the **Cape of Good Hope Nature Reserve**, though seven routes have been charted and signposted. These range from the one-hour Kanonkop Trail on the eastern side to the four-hour (one-way) Good Hope Coastal Walk that takes you along the western shoreline to the wreck-site of the good ship *Phyllisia*. A map of the trail network is available at the reserve's entrance. About 20km (12 miles) of tar and gravel roads are also open to mountain bikers; for information contact Day-trippers: ☎ (021) 511 4766 ✆ (021) 511 4768

Walking Tours
City Centre Stroll
(Map B–F3/4)

Perhaps the most pleasant of the city's several piazzas is the graceful and leafy **Greenmarket Square**, where fruit and vegetable growers once marketed their wares. From Monday to Saturday it is crammed to its limits with umbrella-shaded street-traders' stalls heavy with bric-a-brac, craftwork, creative clothing, leatherware, costume jewellery, fire-sale junk and, occasionally, genuine antiques.

Girding the small square are some very attractive buildings, notably the Gothic-style **Metropolitan Methodist church** and the **Old Town House**, built in the 1750s to house the Burgher Senate (city council) and the Burgher Watch, a kind of police force cum fire-fighting squad. On view inside, beneath the star-spangled dome, are fine works of art including the Michaelis Collection, consisting of some 100 master-pieces of old Flemish and Dutch schools.

Running south to north through the city centre is **St George's Mall**, once congested with traffic but now paved and reserved for pedestrians with time and a little money to spare. There are upmarket shops and arcades to either side, as well as bistros, kiosks, street stalls and buskers on the paved area.

Long Street, which runs parallel to St George's Mall, was the liveliest part of 19th-century Cape Town and it still draws bargain-hunters, serendipity shoppers and bibliophiles with its antique and junk outlets, pawnshops and second-hand bookshops.

Near the corner of Hout and Long Streets is the **Sendinggestig**, the Missionary Meeting House museum and one of the city's more elegant edifices. Inside you'll see a handsome hall, galleries of yellowwood and stinkwood resting on Ionian columns, a splendid pulpit (Chinese Chippendale) and pipe-organ, oak pews and teak balconies, and also displays of early missionary work at the Cape.

The upper end of the thoroughfare boasts some charming late-Victorian buildings (among them the striking-looking **Blue Lodge**), many of which have received facelifts and now stand proud in their filigreed glory. While heading south towards the famous Long Street baths (heated pool, massage, Turkish steam) at the top end of the street, keep an eye open for the **Palm Tree** and **Dorp Street mosques**.

Table Mountain Walks

Table Mountain offers numerous walks and climbs. Some of the established paths are gentle enough (it is a two-hour uphill walk from the back, or southern slopes, of the mountain), others are more strenuous, and some down-right dangerous. All the routes should be treated with respect. It is easy to get lost, which can be a frightening experience if the weather turns nasty – as it can do, suddenly and without any warning at all. Invest in a good map and guidebook (available in city bookshops); choose a route that is well within your

> **Mountain Dassies**
> Table Mountain is home to a myriad dassies, or hyraxes, little rodent-like creatures which live among the rocks and cliffs, and provide meals for the birds of prey. Despite their small size and insignificant looks, the species can claim surprisingly noble lineage – their nearest relative is the mighty elephant! The two animals have followed widely divergent evolutionary routes, but they do have some features in common, including the structure of their feet and teeth, their reproductive cycles, and their blood serology.

Below: *One of the hiking trails in Table Mountain's deep ravines.*

<u>Touring</u>
<u>Coach tours:</u>
Hylton Ross Tours
☎ (021) 438 1500
📠 (021) 438 2919
Mother City Tours
☎ (021) 448 3817
📠 (021) 448 3844
Windward Coach Charter
☎ (021) 790 2012
📠 (021) 790 3633
Specialized Tours
☎ (021) 425 3259
📠 (021) 425 3329
Grassroots Tours
☎ (021) 706 1006
📠 (021) 705 0798
Sunchaser Tours
☎ 082 460 7142
<u>Cycling tours:</u>
Bikeabout Cycle Tours
☎ (021) 511 4766
Mike Hopkins Kawasaki
☎ (021) 423 8461
📠 (021) 424 5428
<u>Helicopter trips:</u>
Civair
☎ (021) 419 5182
📠 (021) 419 5183
CHC Helicopters
☎ (021) 934 0560
📠 (021) 934 0568
Sport Helicopters
☎ (021) 419 5907
📠 (021) 419 4044
<u>Canoeing:</u>
Felix Unite River Adventures
☎ (021) 683 6433
📠 (021) 712 5241
River Rafters
☎ (021) 712 5094
📠 (021) 712 5241
<u>Balloon tours:</u>
Winelands Hot-Air Ballooning
☎ (021) 863 3192

physical capability; do not stray from the path; and, if it's your first trip, arrange to make it in the company of someone who knows the terrain.

Nature Walks

The **Cape of Good Hope Nature Reserve** (*see* page 19) and **Kirstenbosch National Botanical Garden** (*see* page 21) offer many relaxing trails for lovers of plants and scenic slendour. **Cecilia forest**, which fringes the enchanting Constantia Valley, **Silvermine Nature Reserve** (*see* page 40), **Tokai forest** and **Newlands forest** (*see* page 27) offer easier walks with excellent views.

Organized Tours

Cape Town offers the visitor a variety of interesting tours, ranging from **coach tours** of the city to **helicopter trips** and **hot-air balloon tours** over the Peninsula. For more

information, contact the various tourism offices, or see the panel on the opposite page for details.

Topless bus tours of the city are very popular, offering uninterrupted views of all the sights and attractions. **Boat cruises** to the offshore islands are recommended.

Alternative Cape Town

The national constitution protects the rights of gays and lesbians and Cape Town is regarded as the country's 'gay capital'. Official publications include the **Pink Map** and **Cape Town Gay Guide**; bookshops stock *OUTRight*, *Exit*, *Women on Women* and other, less specialized periodicals that give coverage to the gay scene, including the *Cape Review* and *South African City Life*. There's also the **Gay and Lesbian Advice Centre** for more information. Together, these sources yield detailed information on the city's myriad gay-friendly venues and activities – shops, restaurants, cruise-bars, guest-houses, B&Bs, nightspots, film, video and cabaret shows. Key annual events include the exuberant **Masquerade Party** (October), the **Mother City Queer Project** party (December) and the film festival (January/February).

Above: *A topless tourist bus takes visitors up to Signal Hill for magnificent views of the city.*
Opposite: *Much of the Cape Peninsula is wooded, making it ideal for rambles, walks and hikes.*

Nomvuyo's Tours
No-one should spend time in Cape Town without visiting **Khayelitsha**, South Africa's largest township. There are full- and half-day tours where you can experience the sights, sounds and smells of Khayelitsha. Special tours include a shebeen tour, a tour of the craft centres, and an overnight stay at one of the established B&Bs. For details, contact Jenny at
✉ PO Box 51553, V & A Waterfront, 8002,
☎ (021) 465 4585,
📠 (021) 434 0594,
🖳 d6girl@hotmail.com

Right: Victoria Wharf shopping mall in the V & A Waterfront.

Shops

South Africa has a free-market economy and offers the visitor irresistible bargains, from something in gold and diamond (tax-free) at Cape Town's top shopping mall, the V & A Waterfront, or a small thing from a roadside hawker, the current rand value leans heavily in your favour.

The most fascinating things one can buy include a soapstone sculpture from the pavement hawkers, bags, belts and books from flea markets or an ostrich-skin brief-case, crocodile-skin bag, hand-woven rugs and designer jewellery from stylish sub-urban shopping malls. If you are interested in ethnic items, flea markets and curio shops are worth a visit.

On your shopping list you can include woven grass tablemats, ostrich eggs and ostrich feathers, colourful bead necklaces, copperware, ceramics, items made from wool and mohair and African handicrafts.

Shopping hours are generally 08:00–17:00 on weekdays and 08:00–13:00 on Saturdays. Supermarkets and most large shopping centres are also open on Sundays.

Shops

African Image

A wide range of some of the best indigenous African craftwork.
✉ 52 Burg Street,
☎ (021) 423 8385,
📠 (021) 422 1575,
✍ info@
african-image.co.za
🖥 www.
african-image.co.za

Montebello Design Centre

This gem is hidden in leafy Newlands and there are a number of shops selling hand-crafted goods, as well as a nursery, forge, and restaurant set under huge trees.
✉ 31 Newlands Avenue, Newlands,
☎ (021) 685 6445,
📠 (021) 686 7403,
✍ montebello@
netpoint.co.za
🕐 09:00–17:00 Mon–Fri, 10:00–15:00 Sat and Sun.

Cavendish Square

A very large, upmarket shopping complex with a choice of shops and restaurants in the heart of the shopping mecca of Claremont.
✉ Cavendish Street,
☎ (021) 674 3050,
📠 (021) 671 1313,
✍ info@
cavendish.co.za
🖥 www.
cavendish.co.za

Canal Walk

The place to go for choice of shops, but only if your feet are up for all the walking! The largest shopping centre in Africa offers a vast choice of shops. *See page 23 for details.*

V & A Waterfront

The prime shopping destination in Cape Town offering everything from curio shops to fashion boutiques. *See page 15 for details.*

Tyger Valley Centre

Apart from a large number of shops, there is also a massive entertainment complex that includes big-screen videos, video games, cinemas and restaurants.
✉ 1 Willie van Schoor Avenue, Belville,

See page 23 for details.

See page 15 for details.

Weaving Magic
Bhabhathane is the Xhosa word for 'butterfly', symbolizing the colourful success of this self-help weaving scheme. It was launched in the mid-1980s in a desperate effort to beat the local unemployment crisis, and now turns out a range of handmade items, including runners, carpets and tapestries made from mohair and karakul wool. If you don't fancy what's on offer, just sketch your preference and the craftspersons will translate the design into a specially-made woven product.
✉ Verster Street, Paarl, or you can visit the studio at the Ikwhezi centre, Dal Josafat, on the R303.

☎ (021) 914 1822,
📠 (021) 914 1318,
🖥 www.
tygervalley.co.za

Somerset Mall

A stylish shopping destination in the Cape winelands, Somerset Mall continues to draw new customers, attracting them with a multitude of stores and entertainment venues.
⊠ off the N2 highway, Somerset West,
☎ (021) 852 7114/5,
📠 (021) 852 1249,
✆ management@
somerset-mall.co.za
🖥 www.
somerset-mall.co.za

Long Street Shops

Cape Town is famous for its beautiful antiques – from Art Nouveau jewellery to rare books and precious *objets* – many of which can be discovered behind the quaint shop fronts of the original Victorian buildings lining Long Street and its surrounds.
⊠ Long Street,
🕒 daily.

Markets

Many markets take place over weekends and public holidays, mostly in the suburbs. At craft markets you'll find a splendid variety of original wares ranging from yellow-wood furniture, hand-blown glass, pottery, basketry and inventive jewellery to carpets, tapestries and trendy clothing.

Greenmarket Square

This cobbled square is a vibrant melting-pot of cultural diversity, bustling with shoppers and bargain-hunters, filled with fleamarket stalls and buskers, and

Below: *The filigreed charm of Long Street. Many of the building's facades are being restored and now house interesting shops.*

fringed by art dealers, gold and diamond merchants, sushi bars, internet cafés, fashion emporiums and historical buildings.

⊠ *Greenmarket Square,*
🕐 *Mon–Fri and Sat mornings.*

The Blue Shed Art and Craft Market, and the Red Shed Craft Workshop

A wide range of ceramics, jewellery, textiles, basketware, township art and candles are on sale.

⊠ *V & A Waterfront,*
🕐 *Sat and Sun.*

Constantia Craft Market

⊠ *Kendall Road, Constantia.*

Groot Constantia Craft Market

⊠ *on the Groot Constantia estate.*

Craft in the Park

⊠ *in the Rondebosch Park (corner of Campground and Sandown roads, near the Common).*

Green Point Stadium Craft Market

⊠ *Sea Point,* 🕐 *Sun.*

Kirstenbosch Craft Market

⊠ *on the corner of Kirstenbosch and Rhodes Drive, opposite the entrance to the botanical gardens.*

Grand Parade

⊠ *in front of the City Hall, Darling Street,* 🕐 *Wed and Sat.*

St George's Mall

Stalls selling clothing, bags and African crafts.

⊠ *St George's Mall.*

Antique Market

⊠ *Church Street.*

Above: *Umbrellas shade the busy street-traders on Greenmarket Square.*

Noordhoek Arts and Crafts

Artists and craftpersons welcome visitors to their studios at Noordhoek. Alternatively, you can view (and buy) their works at **Chapman's Bay Trading Centre** and at the **Noordhoek Art Gallery**, both on Beach Road. The Beach Road centre also includes the pleasant Red Herring restaurant and Adagio Café. Nearby, off the main road, is **Noordhoek Farm Village**, well worth visiting for its appealing architecture, its sculpture garden, farm stall, pub (the Nag's Head) and a dozen or so imaginatively stocked speciality shops.

Above: *The Houw Hoek Inn, beyond Sir Lowry's Pass.*

Country Getaway
If you enjoy peace and quiet, the **Houw Hoek Inn** is for you.
✉ PO Box 95, Grabouw, 7160
☎ (028) 284 9646
📠 (028) 284 9112
📧 houwhoek@iafrica.com
💻 www.houwhoekinn.co.za

Famous Visitor
In Cape Town's early days, many of the attractive hotels catered for the more well-to-do visitors. Among these was the grand new **Mount Nelson Hotel** (*see page 56*), which hosted a veritable who's-who of Britain during the Anglo-Boer war (1899–1902), including a young, dashing **Winston Churchill**, of London's *Morning Post*.

WHERE TO STAY

The best **hotels** are of an international standard. A voluntary grading system, covering all types of accommodation, is in operation; ratings range from one to five stars.

Many of the better establishments are controlled by one or other of the large hotel chains; most offer packages, out-of-season, family rates and other inducements. The more prominent of the hotel groups are Sun International, Southern Sun/Holiday Inn, City Lodge (very few frills, competitive rates) and Karos. Protea is a management rather than proprietary enterprise, and its hotels have kept their individual yet professional characters.

Visitors also have a wide choice of **guest houses** in and around the Cape Peninsula. (Publications available from bookshops).

The outlying areas are well endowed with good **country getaways** – restful little lodges tucked away in the valleys. Most offer supreme comfort, some are highly sophisticated in terms of appointment and cuisine, and all are informal and friendly.

Guest farms are ideal for a healthy family holiday. Stay in the farmhouse or in a chalet or cottage on the property, and take part in the life of the ranch, farm or wine estate.

Increasingly popular **self-catering** options throughout the wider region are numerous and varied, ranging from basic holiday apartments and cottages to well-appointed, luxurious resort-type chalets.

Bed-and-breakfast accommodation is becoming an ever more popular option, and many Capetonians are making their homes available to visitors. Ask your travel agent or Cape Town Tourism for details.

City Centre

Cape Swiss

(Map B–E5)

This hotel has a pleasant setting on the lower slopes of Table Mountain.

✉ Kloof Street,

☎ (021) 423 8190,

📠 (021) 426 1795.

Capetonian

(Map B–G3)

Located near the central area and the harbour, serving excellent seafood.

✉ Pier Place, Heerengracht,

☎ (021) 405 5670,

📠 (021) 405 5660.

Holiday Inn (Cape Town)

(Map B–F4)

This city centre hotel is linked to the main shopping area by concourse; it has several restaurants on the premises, serving traditional Cape dishes as well as French cuisine and a carvery.

✉ Strand Street,

☎ (021) 488 5100,

📠 (021) 423 8875,

💻 www. holiday-inn.co.za

City Lodge – V & A

(Map B–G2)

Located at the gateway to the Waterfront (walking distance from city centre).

✉ corner of Dock and Alfred roads,

☎ (021) 419 9450,

📠 (021) 419 0460,

📧 clva@resv.co.za

💻 www. citylodge.co.za

Holiday Inn Garden Court – De Waal Drive

(Map B–F5)

Close to Company's Garden, popular with leisure and business travellers.

✉ Mill Street, Gardens,

☎ (021) 465 1311,

📠 (021) 461 6648,

📧 higcctdewaal@ southernsun.com

💻 www. southernsun.com

Woodlands Guest House (Map B–F6)

Enjoy warm hospitality, African ambience and an amazing garden in this graceful Victorian guest house in the heart of Cape Town.

✉ 6 Upper Orange Street, Oranjezicht,

☎/📠 (021) 461 3951,

📧 jan_roos@ mweb.co.za

💻 www.members. africa-adventure. org/w/woodlands

Park Inn Greenmarket Square

(Map B–F4)

This hotel is conveniently located right in the central city, overlooking the charming piazza.

✉ Greenmarket Square,

☎ (021) 423 2050,

📠 (021) 423 2059,

💻 www.parkinn.com

Holiday Inn Garden Court – St George's Mall

(Map B–G3)

It has a central location, situated on the pedestrian mall close to the shops and city attractions.

✉ St George's Mall,

☎ (021) 419 0808,

📠 (021) 419 6010,

📧 reservations.st. georges@mweb.co.za

💻 www. africanskyhotels.com

Mount Nelson

(Map B–E5)

World-renowned elegant luxury hotel. Personal service, superb cuisine.

⊠ 76 Orange Street,
☎ (021) 423 1000,
℡ (021) 424 7472,
✆ reservations@ mountnelson.co.za
🖳 www. mountnelson.co.za

Town House

(Map B–F4)

On the fringes of the city centre; a quietly tasteful hotel.

⊠ 60 Corporation Street,
☎ (021) 465 7050,
℡ (021) 465 3891,
✆ hotel@ townhouse.co.za
🖳 www. townhouse.co.za

Tulbagh Hotel

(Map B–G3)

This quiet establishment is located in an attractive central city square.

⊠ 9 Tulbagh Square,
☎ (021) 421 5140,
Central reservations
☎ 0800 11 9000,
℡ (021) 421 4648,

✆ tinfo@ cpthotels.co.za
🖳 www. cpthotels.co.za

Waterfront

Breakwater Lodge

(Map D–B2)

Vibrant setting, good value for money.

☎ (021) 406 1911,
℡ (021) 406 1070,
✆ reserve@bwl.co.za
🖳 www.bwl.co.za

Victoria & Alfred Hotel

(Map D–C2)

Converted historic harbour building.

⊠ Pierhead,
☎ (021) 419 6677,
℡ (021) 419 8955,
✆ res@vahotel.co.za
🖳 www.vahotel.co.za

The Table Bay

(Map D–E1)

The ultimate in five-star luxury and comfort, excellent cuisine, superlative views over mountain or bay, in-house spa.

☎ (021) 406 5000,
℡ (021) 406 5767,
✆ tbhres@sunint.co.za
🖳 www. suninternational.com

Cape Grace

(Map D–C3)

Small luxury hotel, own quay, hospitable.

⊠ West Quay Road,
☎ (021) 410 7100,
℡ (021) 419 7622,
✆ info@ capegrace.com
🖳 www. capegrace.com

Atlantic Seaboard

Ambassador Hotel and Executive Suites

(Map B–B4)

Spectacularly set on water's edge.

⊠ 34 Victoria Road, Bantry Bay,
☎ (021) 439 6170,
℡ (021) 439 6336,
✆ reservations@ ambassador.co.za
🖳 www. ambassador.co.za

The Bay

(Map C–B1)

Splendid luxury, spectacular seaviews.

⊠ 69 Victoria Road, Camps Bay,
☎ (021) 430 4444,
℡ (021) 438 4455,
✆ res@thebay.co.za
🖳 www.thebay.co.za

Protea Hotel President

(Map B–B4)
Exquisitely sited on rocky seafront.
✉ 4 Alexander Road, Sea Point,
☎ (021) 434 8111,
Central reservations
☎ 0800 11 9000,
📠 (021) 434 9991,
✆ sales@ presidenthotel.co.za
🖥 www. proteahotels.com/ president

☎ (021) 439 6010,
📠 (021) 434 0809,
✆ ctritz@iafrica.com
🖥 www. africanskyhotels.com

Above: *The gracious Mount Nelson Hotel is situated close to the city centre.*

The Peninsula All-Suite

(Map B–B4)
Overlooking the bay, stunning ocean views.
✉ 313 Beach Road, Sea Point,
☎ (021) 430 7777,
toll-free 0800 22 4433,
📠 (021) 430 7776,
✆ hotel@ peninsula.co.za
🖥 www. peninsula.co.za

Ritz Inn

(Map B–D2)
Near the seafront; noted for revolving restaurant.
✉ Main Road, Sea Point,

Winchester Mansions

(Map B–C2)
Family hotel on seafront.
✉ 221 Beach Road, Sea Point,
☎ (021) 434 2351,
📠 (021) 434 0215,
✆ sales@ winchester.co.za
🖥 www. winchester.co.za

Suburbs and Peninsula

City Lodge GrandWest

(Map C–D1)
Cape-Dutch style of architecture, part of the casino complex.

Prison Hotel

The Waterfront's Breakwater Lodge and MBA campus is a complex with a difference: it's part of the original, old Breakwater Prison, built in 1859 (and later extended) to house long-term convicts assigned to work on Table Bay's dock construction programme. The prison's original facade and courtyard have been retained, but the rest of the complex was rebuilt to create the modern, 300-bedroom lodge as well as premises for the University of Cape Town's Graduate School of Business. The school's facilities include seven lecture theatres, 50 seminar rooms, a high-tech library, restaurant, cafeteria and bar.

⊠ GrandWest Casino and Theme Park, off Vanguard Drive,
☎ (021) 535 3611,
✆ (021) 535 3622,
⌂ clgw@
citylodge.co.za
🖳 www.
citylodge.co.za

Vineyard Hotel
(Map C–C2)
This hotel is in a historic country house, located in a lovely quiet setting.
⊠ Colinton Road, Newlands,
☎ (021) 683 3044,
✆ (021) 683 3365,
⌂ hotel@
vineyard.co.za
🖳 www.
vineyard.co.za

Holiday Inn Garden Court – Newlands
(Map C–C2)
Close to Newlands rugby and cricket grounds.
⊠ Main Road, Newlands,
☎ (021) 683 6562,
✆ (021) 683 6794,
⌂ higcctnewlands@
southernsun.com
🖳 www.
southernsun.com

Alphen Hotel
(Map C–C2)
An 18th-century manor house in a spectacular setting.
⊠ Alphen Drive, Constantia,
☎ (021) 794 5011,
✆ (021) 794 5710,
⌂ reservations@
alphen.co.za
🖳 www.alphen.co.za

The Cellars-Hohenort Country House
(Map C–C2)
This luxury hotel is situated in spacious grounds.
⊠ Brommersvlei Road, Constantia,
☎ (021) 794 2137,
✆ (021) 794 2149,
⌂ cellars@
relaischateaux.com
🖳 www.
collectionmcgrath.com

Lord Nelson Inn
(Map C–C4)
Old-fashioned hospitality, beautifully appointed rooms, excellent service.
⊠ 58 St George's Street, Simon's Town,
☎ (021) 786 1386,
✆ (021) 786 1009,
⌂ nsnelson@
mweb.co.za
🖳 www.simonstown.
com/hotels/lordnelson/

Greenways Hotel
(Map C–C2)
Private establishment, located in a historic Cape house.
⊠ 1 Torquay Avenue, Claremont,
☎ (021) 761 1792,
✆ (021) 761 0878,
⌂ gm@
greenways.co.za
🖳 www.
greenways.co.za

Courtyard at the Cape
(Map C–C1)
Cape Dutch homestead dating to 1700s.
⊠ Liesbeeck Avenue, Mowbray,
☎ (021) 448 3929,
✆ (021) 448 5494,
⌂ cyct.resv@
citylodge.co.za
🖳 www.
citylodge.co.za

Stellenbosch
Devon Valley Protea
(Map A–D4)
Country hotel set amid the vineyards.

✉ *Devon Valley Road,*
☎ *(021) 865 2012,*
📠 *(021) 865 2610,*
⌨ *devon@iafrica.com*
💻 *www.*
devonvalleyhotel.com

D'Ouwe Werf

(Map G–B3)

Small, historic and very charming.

✉ *30 Church Street,*
☎ *(021) 887 4608 or 887 1608,*
📠 *(021) 887 4626,*
⌨ *ouwewerf@ iafrica.com*
💻 *www.*
ouwewerf.com

Stellenbosch Hotel

(Map G–B3)

Known for its all-round excellence.

✉ *162 Dorp Street,*
☎ *(021) 887 3644,*
📠 *(021) 887 3673.*

Lanzerac Hotel

(Map A–D4)

Gracious, historic atmosphere.

✉ *Lanzerac Road,*
☎ *(021) 887 1132,*
📠 *(021) 887 2310,*
⌨ *info@ lanzerac.co.za*
💻 *www.*
lanzerac.co.za

Bon Esperance

(Map G–C3)

Graceful Victorian house, lovely garden.

✉ *17 Van Riebeeck Street,*
☎ *(021) 887 0225,*
📠 *(021) 887 8328,*
⌨ *stay@ bonneesperance.com*
💻 *www.*
bonneesperance.com

Somerset West

Lord Charles Hotel

(Map A–D5)

This is arguably one of the best luxury hotels in South Africa.

✉ *corner Stellenbosch and Faure roads,*
☎ *(021) 855 1040,*
📠 *(021) 855 1107,*
💻 *www.*
the-lord-charles.co.za

Paarl

Grande Roche

(Map F–A3)

Luxury hotel among vineyards: interna-tional standards.

☎ *(021) 863 2727,*
📠 *(021) 863 2220,*
⌨ *reserve @granderoche.co.za*
💻 *www.*
granderoche.co.za

Berghof

(Map F–A1)

State-of-the-art guesthouse with beautiful pool.

✉ *20 Monte Christo Avenue,*
☎ *(021) 871 1099,*
📠 *(021) 872 6126,*
⌨ *berghof@icon.co.za*
💻 *www.*
berghof-paarl.com

Franschhoek

Le Ballon Rouge

(Map H–B2)

A stylish and up-market establishment.

✉ *7 Reservoir Street,*
☎ *(021) 876 2651,*
📠 *(021) 876 3743,*
⌨ *info@ ballon-rouge.co.za*
💻 *www.*
ballon-rouge.co.za

Le Quartier Francais

(Map H–B2)

This is the ultimate in luxury, with a superb restaurant.

✉ *16 Huguenot Street,*
☎ *(021) 876 2151,*
📠 *(021) 876 3105,*
⌨ *res@lqf.co.za*
💻 *www.*
lequartier.co.za

Traditional Desserts
Koeksister: Either cumin-flavoured oval of plaited dough coated with coconut or a deep-fried dough 'twist' soaked in syrup.
Konfyt: Sweet preserves.
Melktert: or 'milk tart'. Cinnamon-coated baked custard on a thin, pastry base.

EATING OUT
What to Eat

Cape Town's myriad restaurants offer the full range of food styles – from the classic to the exotic. Some areas with especially heavy concentrations of eateries are the new big mall and leisure developments located in the northern areas, as well as the V & A Waterfront, and the southern suburban stretch from Rondebosch through to Claremont.

The local line-fish, crayfish (rock lobster) and *perlemoen* (abalone) are usually excellent, though the shellfish tends to be expensive. Antelope venison (including springbok pie) is something of a speciality, and ostrich steaks are becoming an increasingly popular menu item.

Traditional **Cape country fare**, available in selected restaurants, evolved among the rural Afrikaner communities. Common ingredients of the meal include tender Karoo lamb, sweet potatoes, cinnamon-

Below: *Typical Cape fare – kebabs,* potjie *and* pap.

flavoured pumpkin, sweetcorn fritters, and, for dessert, milk tart, *koeksisters* and a selection of sticky preserves which are known as *konfyt*.

Above: *A traditional Cape Malay feast.*

Rather tastier and less stodgy is **Malay cuisine**, introduced by the early slaves from Indonesia and famed for its aromatic *boboties* (curried meatloaf topped with savoury custard), *bredies* (fragrant stews, usually of mutton, with potatoes and vegetables, although *waterblommetjie bredie* is a more piquant variety made from a type of indigenous water lily), spicy *samoosas* and many gooey desserts. The traditional style has been refined over the centuries, taking on some elements of early Dutch, French Huguenot and Indian cooking.

Outdoor entertainment in Cape Town invariably centres around the **braai** or braaivleis; this is usually a standard barbecue of meats such as long-marinated lamb, venison, beef, chicken, spicy *boerewors* ('farmer's sausage'), served with potatoes baked in foil, and a selection of salads. The men invariably do the cooking, which is considered to be something of an art form. Charcoal, wood or both are used for fuel, the wood imparting a distinctive and tasty flavour to the food.

Also very popular is *potjiekos* – a flavourful stew that is cooked gently for several hours and sometimes even days in a giant cast-iron pot over an open fire.

Traditional Foods
Biltong: Air-dried spiced meat.
Bobotie: Curried meatloaf topped with savoury custard.
Boerewors: Spicy, coriander-flavoured 'farmer's sausage'.
Braai: 'braaivleis', a barbecue.
Bredie: Fragrant stew, with potatoes, onions and sometimes vegetables.
Crayfish: Rock lobster.
Mielie: Sweetcorn; corn-on-the-cob.
Pap: Maize-meal.
Perlemoen: Abalone.
Potjiekos: Slow-simmering stew usually cooked over an open fire in a large three-legged pot.
Snoek: A firm-fleshed, strongly-flavoured fish, good for smoking and braaing.
Sosatie: A skewer of curry-marinated meat.

Wine Exports
There are many experts
who will send wine
home or abroad for you:
Manuka Fine Wines,
✉ Steenberg Village
Shopping Centre, Tokai,
☎ (021) 701 2046,
🖥 www.manuka.co.za
**Vaughan Johnson's
Wine Shop,**
✉ V & A Waterfront,
☎ (021) 419 2121,
📠 (021) 419 0040.
**The Vinyard Connec-
tion,** ✉ Stellenbosch,
☎ (021) 884 4360.
**Oom Samie se
Winkel,** ✉ 84 Dorp
Street, Stellenbosch,
☎ (021) 887 2612.
Steven Rom,
✉ Sea Point,
☎ (021) 439 6043.
**Wine-Of-The-Month-
Club,** ✉ Claremont,
☎ (021) 657 8100/
8181, 📠 671 4992.
**Picardi Fine Wine and
Spirits,** ✉ Foreshore,
Cape Town, ☎ (021)
425 1639/64.

Traditional **African cuisine** does not yet appear on very many restaurant menus, but this is now starting to change, as more and more innovative chefs have started introducing elements of African cuisine to their dishes. For most black people in South Africa, eating remains a practical necessity; the ordinary meal of the day in the townships tends to be a no-nonsense affair in which *pap* (maize-meal), boiled meat or cabbage, or samp and beans is the order of the day. But living standards throughout the country are slowly improving.

What to Drink

There are some 4000 locally produced **wines** on the market, from delicate dry whites to full-bodied reds. All of them are drinkable, many are noteworthy, and a few are truly memorable – the better ones are fast gaining an international reputation. The best way to explore the range of wines available is to embark on one or more of the world-famous **wine routes** (*see* pages 76–79). Selected bookshops as well as some liquor stores stock informative guides to the wine-growing areas and the many labels on offer.

A very popular drink in the Cape is the distinctively fragrant **rooibos tea**, which is made from the leaves of an indigenous herbal bush found near Clanwilliam.

Where to Eat

There are restaurants for all preferences and pockets in Cape Town; the menus on offer range from traditional Cape fare and seafood, through Mediterranean, Cajun, Italian, Chinese, Indian and Mexican to French *haute cuisine*. Several eateries also double as taverns that occasionally feature live music and entertainment. The Sports Café chain of pubs and restaurants combines conviviality with sporting interest: television sets beam local and international events while patrons watch, eat, drink and make merry.

Cape Town's coffee bars and bistros cater for those with more sophisticated tastes, while fast-food outlets offer a wide variety of 'food to go'.

The West Coast is especially famed for its delicious seafood, freshly caught and often enjoyed in open-air restaurants that are noted for their wonderfully informal sociability.

> **Open-Air Eating**
> Among the best-known of these alfresco eateries are: Die Melkbosskerm, Melkbosstrand; Die Strandloper near Langebaan; the Breakwater Boma at Saldanha Bay and, further north at Lambert's Bay, Muisbosskerm.

Opposite: *La Concorde is the headquarters of the KWV wine enterprise in Paarl.*
Below: *Indulgent wine tasting at Nederburg.*

City Centre

Africa Café

Ethnic dishes from throughout Africa.
✉ 108 Shortmarket Street,
☎ (021) 422 0221,
📠 (021) 422 0482,
✆ africafe@iafrica.com
🖳 www.africacafe.co.za

Anatoli

Turkish fare in Middle Eastern surrounds.
✉ Napier Street,
☎ (021) 419 2501.

Bacini's

A delicious selection of pizzas and pasta.
✉ 177 Kloof Street, Gardens,
☎ (021) 423 6668.

Bukhara

Excellent North Indian cuisine, open for lunch and dinner.
✉ 33 Church Street,
☎ (021) 424 0000.

Floris Smit Huis

International focus.
✉ corner Church and Loop Streets,
☎ (021) 423 3414/5,
📠 (021) 423 3415.

The Grill Room

Elegant, old-style service, continental cuisine.
✉ Mount Nelson Hotel,
☎ (021) 483 1000,
📠 (021) 483 1947.

La Brasserie

Varied menus in a modern setting.
✉ St George's Hotel corner Riebeeck Street and St George's Mall,
☎ (021) 419 0808,
📠 (021) 419 7010.

Maria's

Small Greek restaurant; excellent fare.
✉ Dunkley Square, 31 Barnet Street,
☎ (021) 461 8887.

Miller's Thumb

Fish fare.
✉ 10b Kloofnek Road, Tamboerskloof,
☎ (021) 424 3838.

Aubergine

Superb service, varied menu (with emphasis on Cape and German dishes).
✉ 39 Barnet Street, Gardens,
☎ (021) 465 4909,
📠 (021) 461 3781,
✆ aubergin@mweb.co.za
🖳 www.aubergine.co.za

Rozenhof

Classic menu, variety of fine food.
✉ 18 Kloof Street, Gardens,
☎ (021) 424 1968,
📠 (021) 423 6058,
✆ rozenhofrestaurant@mweb.co.za

Mama Africa

African continental food, lively bar.
✉ 178 Long Street,
☎ (021) 424 8634,
📠 (021) 424 9457.

Vasco da Gama Taverna

A friendly Portuguese restaurant, attractively downmarket.
✉ 3 Alfred Street,
☎ (021) 425 2157.

Savoy Cabbage

Eclectic cuisine, very trendy place.
✉ 101 Hout Street,
☎ (021) 424 2626,
📠 (021) 424 3366,
✆ savoycab@iafrica.com

Waterfront

Alabama Floating Restaurant

Wine and dine while cruising the harbour.
⊠ 6 Quay 5, V & A Waterfront,
☎ 082 672 9621.

Aldo's

Classic Italian regional cuisine, as well as seafood specialities.
⊠ Victoria Wharf Shopping Centre,
☎ (021) 421 7874,
📠 (021) 421 7876.

Dodge City Diner

Casual 1950s style.
⊠ Victoria Wharf Shopping Centre,
☎ (021) 418 1445,
🖰 dodge@mweb.co.za

Ferryman's Tavern

Converted railway shed; brewery next door; splendid beer.
⊠ East Pier Road,
☎ (021) 419 7748,
📠 (021) 421 4463,
🖰 ferrymans@mweb.co.za

Green Dolphin

Seafood, pasta. Good jazz played nightly.

⊠ Alfred Mall, Pierhead,
☎ (021) 421 7471/5,
📠 (021) 421 7480,
🖰 green-dolphin@mweb.co.za
🖳 www.greendolphin.co.za

Hildebrand

This restaurant is a popular lunch venue; dinner reservations are essential. Excellent service; Continental cuisine.
⊠ Pierhead,
☎ (021) 425 3385,
📠 (021) 421 4089,
🖰 hildebrand@mweb.co.za
🖳 www.hildebrand.co.za

Above: *Inside one of the Waterfront's many restaurants.*

Sunny Skies and Braaivleis

The **braai**, one of South Africa's more lasting traditions, is a barbeque featuring well-marinated meats, and spicy **boerewors** (farmer's sausage), usually accompanied by beer, wine and a variety of salads. South Africa's sunny climate is perfect for these gatherings, and on weekends tantalizing aromas of sizzling meat fill the air across suburbia.

The Healthy Rooibos Leaf

The needle-sharp leaves of the rooibos shrub, which flourishes in the uplands around Clanwilliam, produce an aromatic herbal tea that is fast gaining popularity beyond South Africa's borders. For centuries the leaf has been prized for its medicinal properties and a hot cup of the beverage certainly does have a soothing effect. There appears good reason to believe it helps relieve insomnia, nervous tension, stomach cramps, colic in babies, some allergies and, when applied directly, skin disorders such as nappy rash.

Below: *A refreshing halt on the drive through Constantia.*

Morton's on the Wharf

Echoes of New Orleans, with tasty Cajun food and blackened grills.
⊠ *Victoria Wharf Shopping Centre,*
☎ *(021) 418 3633,*
℡ *(021)418 3637,*
⌁ *mortons@ kristensen.co.za*
🖳 *www.mortons.co.za*

Panama Jack's Tavern

Informal seafood eatery.
⊠ *Elliot Basin, Table Bay Harbour,*
☎ *(021) 447 3992,*
℡ *(021) 447 5471,*
⌁ *panamajacks@ mweb.co.za*

Quay 4

Lively outdoor tavern downstairs, smarter restaurant upstairs.
☎ *(021) 419 2008,*
℡ *(021) 421 2056,*
⌁ *quay4@ kristensen.co.za*
🖳 *www.quay4.co.za*

The Greek Fisherman

Seafood fresh off the grill; great calamari.
⊠ *157 Victoria Wharf,*
☎ *(021) 418 5411,*
℡ *(021) 418 5412,*
⌁ *info@ greekfisherman.co.za*
🖳 *www. greekfisherman.co.za*

Ocean Basket

Seafood buffet, as well as vegetarian and Halaal specialities.
⊠ *222 Victoria Wharf,*
☎ *(021) 419 4300,*
℡ *(021) 425 1840.*

Bayfront Blu

Seafood and African dishes, superb views.
⊠ *Two Oceans Aquarium,*
☎ *(021) 419 9068,*
℡ *(021) 419 9221,*
⌁ *bayfrontblu@ icon.co.za*

Suburbs and Peninsula

Au Jardin

Elegant, serves delicious French cuisine.

✉ Vinyard Hotel, Colinton Road, Newlands,
☎ (021) 683 1520,
✆ (021) 683 3365/6.

Blues

Fine Californian and Mediterranean food superlatively served; varied menu.

✉ 69 Victoria Road, Camps Bay,
☎ (021) 438 2040/1,
✆ (021) 438 3238.

Buitenverwachting

Deluxe, award-winning restaurant. Very formal.

✉ Klein Constantia Road, Constantia,
☎ (021) 794 3522,
✆ (021) 794 1351.

Europa

Situated in an elegant old house, serving seafood specialities.

✉ 78 Regent Road, Sea Point,
☎ (021) 439 2820,
✆ (021) 439 3369.

Peddlars on the Bend

Hearty country fare, rural surrounds, excellent value, very popular.

✉ Spaanschemat River Road, Constantia,
☎ (021) 794 7747,
✆ (021) 794 2730.

Constantia Uitsig Restaurant

Fine Mediterranean Provençal cuisine; highly recommended.

✉ Spaanschemat River Road, Constantia,
☎ (021) 794 4480,
✆ (021) 794 3105.

The Brass Bell

Popular with the locals; overlooks the harbour and serves excellent seafood.

✉ Main Road, Kalk Bay,
☎ (021) 788 5456/55,
✆ (021) 788 3430.

Black Marlin

Good seafood eating with bayside views.

✉ Main Road, Miller's Point (near Simon's Town),
☎ (021) 786 1621,
✆ (021) 786 3876.

Lord Nelson Inn

Cozy, colonial eatery; good seafood.

✉ 58 St George's Street, Simon's Town,
☎ (021) 786 1386,
✆ (021) 786 1009,
✆ nsnelson@mweb.co.za

Red Herring

Quality fare, seafood specialities.

✉ Corner Beach and Pine Roads, Noordhoek,
☎ (021) 789 1783,
✆ (021) 789 2900.

Franschhoek

The Cape's 'food capital' has many fine restaurants.

Haute Cabriere

Set in an underground cellar, serves gourmet lunches.

✉ Cabriere Estate, Pass Road,
☎ (021) 876 3688.

La Maison de Chamonix

Caters for the whole family, cosy environment.

☎ (021) 876 2393,
✆ (021) 876 3691.

La Petite Ferme
Popular venue serving French and South African cuisine.
☎ (021) 876 3016/8,
📞 (021) 876 3624.

Le Ballon Rouge
French-SA fusion.
✉ 7 Reservoir Street,
☎ (021) 876 2651,
📞 (021) 876 3743,
🖎 info@
ballon-rouge.co.za
💻 www.
ballon-rouge.co.za

Le Quartier Français
Innovative dishes, garden views from every table.
✉ 16 Huguenot Road,
☎ (021) 876 2151,
📞 (021) 876 3105,
🖎 res@lfq.co.za
💻 www.
lequartier.co.za

Boschendal
Cape buffet; Le Pique-Nique among the pines; Le Café.
☎ (021) 870 4274,
📞 (021) 874 2137,
🖎 reservations@
boschendal.com
💻 www.
boschendal.com

Paarl
Bosman's
Gourmet cuisine, rated among the country's best.
✉ Grande Roche Hotel, Plantasie Street,
☎ (021) 863 2727,
📞 (021) 863 2220.

Rhebokskloof
Wine estate with three restaurants; small lake featuring black swans.
☎ (021) 869 8606,
📞 (021) 869 8906,
🖎 restaurant@
rhebokskloof.co.za
💻 www.
rhebokskloof.co.za

Lobfti's Restaurant
Cape Dutch farm-house; traditional Cape fare.
✉ Dal Josafat valley,
☎/📞 (021) 868 1535.

Somerset West
Garden Terrace
Superb Cape Malay dishes, carvery and buffet.
✉ Lord Charles Hotel,
☎ (021) 855 1040,
📞 (021) 855 1107.

L'Auberge du Paysan
This top restaurant has won awards for traditional French fare, served in a smart atmosphere.
✉ PO Box 315, Somerset West 7129,
☎ (021) 842 2008,
💻 www.
aubergedupaysan.
co.za

96 Winery Road
The menu at this restaurant shows Cape, Provençal and eastern influences.
✉ Zandberg Farm, Winery Road,
☎ (021) 842 2020,
📞 (021) 842 2050,
💻 www.
96wineryroad.co.za

Stellenbosch
There are so many restaurants and pubs in the town and on surrounding wine farms, that is would be a good idea to obtain the free guide to the area from Cape Town Tourism or the Stellenbosch Tourist Bureau and Wine Route Office.

De Akker

Serves good hearty pub food.

✉ *Dorp Street,*

☎ *(021) 883 3512.*

De Cameron

Fine food from the Italian south.

✉ *50 Plein Street,*

☎ *(021) 883 3331,*

📠 *(021) 883 2553.*

Lanzerac

Rather formal restaurant, serving very good food in a splendidly historic setting.

✉ *Lanzerac Hotel, Stellenbosch,*

☎ *(021) 887 1132,*

📠 *(021) 887 2310,*

📧 *info@ lanzerac.co.za*

💻 *www. lanzerac.co.za*

D'Ouwe Werf

Cape dishes in enchanting courtyard setting.

✉ *30 Church Street,*

☎ *(021) 887 4608/ 887 1608,*

📠 *(021) 887 4626,*

📧 *ouwewerf@ iafrica.com*

💻 *www. ouwewerf.com*

Lord Neethling Restaurant

Splendid Cape homestead; Cape and Continental dishes.

✉ *Polkadraai Road,*

☎ *(021) 883 8966,*

📠 *(021) 883 9803,*

📧 *manny@iafrica.com*

💻 *www. lordneethling.co.za*

The Fishmonger

This eatery serves a wonderful selection of seafood and sushi, and for dessert the *crème brûlée* is incomparable.

✉ *28 Ryneveld Street,*

☎ *(021) 887 7835.*

The Terrace

Pub-style light meals, pleasant aspect.

✉ *Drostdy Centre,*

☎ *(021) 887 1942.*

De Volkskombuis

Traditional Cape cooking.

✉ *Aan-de-Wagen Road,*

☎ *(021) 887 2121,*

📠 *(021) 883 3413,*

📧 *mail@ volkskombuis.co.za*

💻 *www. volkskombuis.co.za*

Some Common Cultivars

WHITE:

• **Chardonnay:** the grape of the world's great white wines.

• **Sauvignon blanc:** SA's best white cultivar, made in new world and French styles.

• **Chenin blanc:** a versatile workhorse, ranging from dry to dessert wines. Also called Steen.

• **Colombard:** easy drinking varietal, also used for brandy.

• **Muscat d'Alexandre:** sweet, heavy mainly dessert wines. Also called Hanepoot.

RED

• **Cabernet Sauvignon:** this classic varietal is widely planted. New and old world styles are made.

• **Pinotage:** SA's 'own' varietal is now achieving fame world-wide.

• **Shiraz:** known for its fine flavour and 'smoky' bouquet.

• **Merlot:** Gaining strength as a stand-alone varietal.

• **Cinsaut:** Used mainly for blending or light easy wines.

GrandWest Casino
✉ 1 Vanguard Drive, Goodwood
☎ (021) 505 7777
📠 (021) 534 1278
📧 mail@sunint.co.za
💻 www.grandwest.co.za

Club Mykonos Casino
☎ (022) 707 6000
📠 (022) 772 2303
📧 clubmyk@mweb.co.za
💻 www.clubmykonos.co.za
🕐 10:00–late, tables: 18:00–late (weekdays), 10:00–late (weekends)

Caledon Casino
✉ 1 Nerina Avenue, Caledon
☎ (028) 214 1271
📠 (028) 214 1270
📧 hotel@caledoncasino.co.za
💻 www.caledoncasino.co.za
🕐 24 hours daily

ENTERTAINMENT
Casinos

South African gaming laws have changed radically during the past few years. Betting on horses has always been legal, but until the mid-1990s casinos were restricted to the old 'homeland' republics and national states. Currently there are over 40 casino-entertainment-hotel complexes operating, being developed or planned in various parts of the country.

There are three popular casinos in the Western Cape. **GrandWest** was the first to open in 2000 and offers many forms of entertainment for both adults and children. **Club Mykonos** (see page 83), a resort complex situated on the West Coast, has been granted a casino licence and continues to draw day visitors from the city. The most recent casino to open its doors is at the **Caledon** spa complex in the Overberg.

All three offer popular games, such as roulette, blackjack and poker, as well as slot machines and other table games.

Theatre and Music

Theatre and music are alive and well in Cape Town. The grander shows – drama, opera, ballet, oratorio and also the occasional lavish musical – are staged at the **Artscape** (Nico Theatre Centre) on the Foreshore. The three auditoriums in the centre are venues for an increasing number of international (imported) shows.

Above: *Artscape, focal point of the performing arts.*
Opposite: *Glittering GrandWest Casino.*

Plays, music and, sometimes, local and experimental drama can be enjoyed at the **Baxter Theatre Complex**, whose two main halls each have a 600-plus capacity. There's also a small studio/workshop.

Fine productions – especially light musical and comic fare – are staged in Camps Bay's revamped **Theatre on the Bay**. There are also a number of smaller, intimate theatres: check the local press for up-to-date details.

Cape Town caters for most tastes in classical music. Evening concerts are performed in ornately Baroque surrounds at the **City Hall** (*see page 36*). Among other, especially pleasant summertime venues are the V & A Waterfront's open-air **Ampitheatre** and the Kirstenbosch gardens in Newlands.

On the southern fringes of Stellenbosch is the **Oude Libertas Centre**, which welcomes visitors to its underground cellar and restaurant. It is best known for Sunday evening concerts in its 430-seat amphitheatre, modelled on the auditoria of ancient Athens and Epidauros. Sit in the enclosure or on the surrounding lawns with a picnic hamper, sipping wine while the music washes over you – a magical experience. Concerts are

---

Artscape
⊠ 10 DF Malan Street, Foreshore
☎ (021) 410 9800
✆ (021) 421 5448
🖅 artscape@artscape.co.za
🖥 www.artscape.co.za

Baxter Theatre Complex
⊠ Main Road, Rondebosch
☎ (021) 685 7880
✆ (021) 689 1880
🖅 mmanim@protem.uct.ac.za
🖥 www.baxter.co.za

Theatre on the Bay
⊠ 1 Link Street, Camps Bay
☎ (021) 438 3301
✆ (021) 438 1998

Oude Libertas
⊠ Oude Libertas Street, Stellenbosch
☎ (021) 809 7000

Above: *An outdoor concert at the Waterfront.*

held from December to March, which are the warm, dry months. The season's programme usually ranges through the spectrum from jazz and the joyous sounds of Africa to Brahms and Beethoven. Drama and ballet also feature occasionally.

The open-air amphitheatre at **Spier Wine Estate**, near Stellenbosch, offers live jazz, classical and light music in summer.

There's plenty of live entertainment – jazz, pop, cabaret – on the night-time scene. Venues and performers change all the time; for the latest information, consult the Cape Town Tourism office, the local media, or the Entertainment and Leisure Guides available from major bookshops. Most of the bigger hotels also offer dinner-dancing.

Cinema

Most of the large shopping centres in the city and suburbs incorporate movie theatres in their entertainment halls. There are two cinema companies which release the latest Hollywood blockbusters: **Nu Metro** and **Ster Kinekor**. Tickets can be purchased at the various cinemas or through the nationwide reservation system, **Computicket**.

A must for Waterfront visitors is the BMW Pavilion, venue for the **IMAX** experience – the world's largest film format. Pin-sharp images projected onto the huge screen (five storeys high), with powerful digital sound, create something close to 'virtual reality', bringing you right into the picture. The impact is quite astonishing.

Spier
✉ off the R310
☎ (021) 809 1100
📠 (021) 809 1134
📧 reservations@ spier.co.za
🖳 www.spier.co.za

Nu Metro Theatres
☎ (021) 419 9700
📠 (021) 419 1327
🖳 www.numetro.co.za

Ster Kinekor Cinemas
☎ 086 030 0222
🖳 www. sterkinekor.co.za

Computicket
☎ 083 915 8000
📧 info@ computicket.com
🖳 www. computicket.com

IMAX Theatre
✉ BMW Pavillion, Portswood Road
☎ (021) 419 7365
📠 (021) 419 7791
📧 imax@ numetro.co.za
🖳 www.imax.co.za

The world-wide IMAX enterprise has over 100 productions in its library. Titles shown at the Waterfront's theatre – which opened in 1994 with *The Blue Planet*, a magnificent space film about earth – include *The Rolling Stones at the Max*, *Everest*, *The Grand Canyon* and *India: Kingdom of the Tiger*.

Annual Events

The **Minstrel (Coon) Carnival**, at New Year, is the first carnival of the year on Cape Town's events calendar. The **J&B Metropolitan Handicap** – the Cape's top horse race (3rd Saturday) – and the **Cape-to-Rio** yacht race (alternate years, *see* panel page 74), are the two major sporting events in January. The month also heralds the opening of **Shakespeare season** at the Maynardville Open-air Theatre, and the **opening of Parliament**.

March hosts the University of Cape Town **Rag Week**, the **Community Chest Carnival** (at Maynardville) and the gruelling **Cape Argus-Pick 'n Pay Cycle Tour**.

The **Two Oceans Marathon** (Easter Sunday) attracts thousands of runners each April. An **Easter Regatta** is also held at Simon's Town.

July and August is the start of the snoek season and a **Snoek Derby** is held in Hout Bay.

Kirstenbosch has its annual **Spring Wild Flower Show**, and the Waterfront its **Wine festival**, in September. The **Whale-watching season** (which starts as early as May) is at its peak in this month.

December is the time for the **Mother City Queer Project Party**, a gay festival.

Events Further Afield
January: Worcester Agricultural Show.
March: Stellenbosch Carnival; Paarl Vineyard Festival; Caledon Beer and Bread Festival.
April: Nederburg Wine Auction; Paarl Nouveau Wine Festival.
June: Worcester Wineland Festival; Paarl Winter Festival (KWV Cathedral Cellar).
July: KWV Berg River Canoe Marathon, Paarl.
August: Robertson Young Wine Show.
September: Robertson Spring Show; Tulbagh Agricultural Show; Villiersdorp Wild Flower Show; Stellenbosch Cultural (music) Festival (sometimes in October); Caledon and Clanwilliam Wild Flower Show.
October: Ceres Wild Flower Show; Robertson Food and Wine Festival; Stellenbosch Food and Wine Festival; Church Street Festival in Tulbagh; Whale Festival in Hermanus.

Below: *The BMW Pavilion, home of the IMAX theatre.*

Above: *A blustery start to the prestigious biannual Cape-to-Rio yacht race.*

The Ocean Racers
Cape Town harbour features as a major station on some of the world's most prestigious yachting routes, including the biannual classic **Cape-to-Rio** race (with international entries), the **Whitbread** round-the-world and the **BOC** single-handed round-the-world races. The premier local round-the-buoys event is **Rothmans Week**, which takes place in Table Bay during the month of December.

Nightclubs, Bars and Discos

Café Vacca Matta
One of the trendiest hotspots in the city. Dancers often perform on the bar counters.
✉ 1a Seeff House, Hans Strijdom Avenue, Foreshore, ☎ (021) 419 5550, ⌂ info@ vaccamatta.com 💻 www.vaccamatta.com

The Fez
Moroccan-style club which plays a wide variety of music, from soul to house music. Themed parties can be arranged.
✉ 38 Hout Street, ☎ (021) 423 1456, ⌂ info@fez.co.za ⌂ www.fez.co.za.

Rhodes House
Very classy, upmarket club in a Cuban/Latin-style setting, with a middle-aged clientele.
✉ 60 Queen Victoria Street, Gardens, ☎ (021) 424 8844/52, 📠 (021) 424 8849, ⌂ info@ rhodeshouse.com 💻 www. rhodeshouse.com

The Shack
The best place to hear alternative music and enjoy a game of pool.
✉ 45B De Villiers Street, ☎ (021) 461 5892.

Mercury Live & Lounge

Popular venue for live rock and alternative music performances.
✉ 43 De Villiers Street,
☎ (021) 465 2106.

The Drum Café

An authentic African experience where you can drum along to the African beat.
✉ 32 Glynn Street, Gardens,
☎ (021) 461 1305.

Five Flies

Fine restaurant and bar which transforms into a trendy club later at night.
✉ 14–16 Keerom Street,
☎ (021) 424 4442,
℡ (021) 423 1048.

169 on Long

A sophisticated venue that offers a selection of smooth music, including jazz.
✉ 169 Long Street,
☎ (021) 426 1107.

The River Club

A popular venue for staging large music events and raves.
✉ Corner Liesbeeck and Observatory Roads, Observatory,
☎ (021) 448 6117,
🖥 www.riverclub.co.za

Perseverance Tavern

Known to the locals as 'Persies', this is one of the city's oldest taverns, with historic vines in the comfortable and popular courtyard area.
✉ 83 Buitenkant Street,
☎ (021) 461 2440.

Dockside

With the largest, most technically advanced dance floor in the country, and equipped with state-of-the-art lasers and lights, this multi-level disco can compete with the most advanced nightclubs in Europe.
✉ Century City Boulevard,
☎ (021) 552 7303,
🕾 info@docksidesuperclub.com
🖥 www.docksidesuperclub.com

Stones Pool Bar

Bar with many pool tables and good music.
✉ 166 Long Street,
🕾 stones@longstreet.co.za

Joburg

A great late-night spot for the truly adventurous; full bar plus pool tables.
✉ 218 Long Street,
☎ (021) 422 0142.

Plum Crazy

A club with an amazing vibe, cozy indoor lounge, open-air chill-out garden, and great sound and lighting.
✉ 94 Long Street,
☎ (021) 422 1368,
℡ (021) 422 1369,
🕾 plumcrazy@longstreet.co.za

Bardelli's

A trendy restaurant by day, it changes to a popular hangout by night. Special theme parties every weekend. Some of the hottest deep-house deejays in town.
✉ 51 Kenilworth Road, Kenilworth,
☎ (021) 683 1423.

EXCURSIONS

Beyond the bleak Cape Flats, to the north and east of Cape Town, the land rises to the splendid upland ranges of the coastal rampart. The mountains – part of what is known as the Cape fold mountains – are high, their lower slopes and the valleys in between are green and fertile, mantled by pastures and orchards and, especially, by vineyards heavy with fruit.

The **Winelands** were the first of the country areas to be occupied by the early white settlers. As the farmers flourished, so they established villages and, from the later 1600s, began enlarging and also beautifying their homes. The first houses here were modest but, with prosperity, took on wings and cellars, lofts, slave quarters and courtyards.

Perhaps the most enjoyable way of exploring this region is via various **wine routes** – wine-tasting and sightseeing itineraries inspired by and modelled on the successful *weinstrassen* of Germany and France's *routes de vin*.

There are around ten of these wine-ways, collectively covering the ground from the Cape Peninsula northeast as far as **Worcester** and **Robertson**, east to take in the **Little Karoo**, and up the western coastal belt, where the **Swartland** and **Olifantsrivier** wineries attract an ever-increasing number of visitors. The routes of **Stellenbosch**, **Franschhoek** and **Paarl** are the best in the Winelands area.

Other places worth a visit are **Hermanus** (whale capital of the Cape), **Langebaan** on the west coast, and the quaint towns along the southern seaboard.

Above: *Strawberry picking in the Stellenbosch area.*
Opposite: *The rounded bulk of Paarl Rock.*

Paarl's Top Wine Farms
Fairview has excellent vintages and is famous for its goat's cheese.
Landskroon is also known for its cheeses, from the estate's prize-winning Jersey cattle.
Backsberg is on the slopes of Simonsberg. It has an especially atmospheric tasting parlour and a small wine museum.
Zandwijk is South Africa's only kosher winery. Cellar tours by arrangement.
Paarl Rock Brandy Cellar gives visitors a view the entire distillation production process; also on offer is an audio-visual presentation, a small museum and tastings.

Paarl

The town of Paarl is noted for some impressive old buildings, an 11km (7-mile) long main street ornamented with jacarandas and oaks, its prominent role in the wine industry, and its close associations with the long, and often controversial, campaign for the recognition of the Afrikaans language (*taal*). On the slopes of the mountain stands the **Taal Monument**, an impressive structure of three linked columns, fountain and soaring spire. Each of these elements symbolizes a debt owed by the language – to the Western world, to the slaves brought in from the East, and to Africa.

The mountain – which you can drive up via a circular road – is the centrepiece of the **Paarlberg Nature Reserve**, a sanctuary for proteas and other *fynbos* plants, wild olives, orchids and patches of natural forest. Various hiking paths, barbecue and picnic spots have been laid out; the small dams of the area are favoured by serious anglers for the unusually large black bass they sustain.

In Taillefert Street is **Laborie**, owned by the **KWV** (Ko-operatieve Wijnbouwers Vereniging), the world's largest cellar complex under one roof.

The grandest of the many wine farms in the Paarl region is **Nederburg**, an elaborately gabled, classic country homestead set in the wide, vineyard-mantled sweep of the Klein Drakenstein area to the east of Paarl.

Paarl
Location: Map F
Distance from Cape Town: 60 km (37 miles)
Tourism Centre:
✉ corner Auret and Main Streets
☎ (021) 872 3829
📠 (021) 872 9376
🖂 paarl@cis.co.za
🖳 www.paarlonline.com

Taal Monument
☎ (021) 863 2800 (restaurant), (021) 872 3441 (Town Museum has information)
🕐 08:00–17:00 daily

Paarlberg Nature Reserve
☎ (021) 872 3658 or 083 275 8893

KWV
✉ 57 Main Street
☎ (021) 807 3911
📠 (021) 807 3000
🖂 customer@kwv.co.za
🖳 www.kwvgroup.co.za

Nederburg
☎ (021) 862 3104
📠 (021) 862 0878
🖳 www.nederburg.co.za

Stellenbosch
Location: Map G
**Distance from Cape
Town:** 50km (31 miles)
Tourism Centre:
⊠ 36 Market Street
☎ (021) 883 3584
📠 (021) 883 8017
📧 eikestad@
iafrica.com
💻 www.
stellenbosch.org.za

Village Museum
⊠ 18 Ryneveld Street
☎ (021) 887 2902
📠 (021) 883 2232
📧 stelmus@
mweb.co.za
💻 www.museum.
org.za/stelmus
🕙 10:00–17:00 Mon–
Sat, 14:00–17:00 Sun
💰 adults R15,
children R2

Opposite: *The
Delaire homestead.*
Below: *Oak-lined
Dorp Street.*

Stellenbosch

South Africa's second oldest town, founded in 1679 and named in honour of **Simon van der Stel**, lies in the green and pleasant Eerste ('first') River valley beneath the heights of the Papegaaiberg, or 'parrot mountain'. The place wears its age with grace: the early townsfolk planted many stately oak trees, created open spaces, built churches and charming little lime-washed homes; later generations added statelier private residences, some fine public edifices and the **University of Stellenbosch**.

Four splendid houses, representing different eras, have been faithfully restored to their original glory and now form Stellenbosch's **Village Museum**, a complex that illuminates the changing domestic scene during the 18th and much of the 19th centuries. Each is furnished in period fashion, its garden filled with the kinds of plants – decorative, medicinal and culinary – that the early owners would have cultivated. The oldest of these houses is **Schreuderhuis**, built in 1709 by a German immigrant, its architecture, décor and simple, rough-hewn furniture matching his humble status. Even more elegant is **Blettermanhuis**, a house which is typical of the late 18th century. **Grosvenor House**, the kind of town house built by patrician Cape families of the early 1800s, is the most elegant of the four, and its garden the most interesting (it houses a permanent exhibition entitled 'Toys of Yesteryear'). Finally there's the home of **O. M. Bergh**, dating from the latter part of the 19th century and Victorian in character.

You'll also find some noteworthy buildings around **Die Braak**, the spacious village green that once served both as a parade ground for the militia and as an arena for the local festivities. Its military origins are evident in the nearby **Kruithuis** (arsenal), which was built in 1777 and is now a national monument housing old weaponry and Dutch East India Company memorabilia.

Stellenbosch has much to offer the wine-lover. Well worth visiting is **Libertas Parva Cellar**, an elegantly gabled Cape Dutch mansion that houses the massive vats, presses and old implements of the **Stellenryck Wine Museum**.

Next door, **Libertas Parva**, once home to the wife of statesman Jan Smuts and social venue for many South African political luminaries, has retained its period character. It also houses the well-known **Rembrandt van Rijn Art Museum** which includes works by some of the country's leading artists.

The 28 cellars and co-operatives on the Stellenbosch wine route are all located on four major roads within a 12km (7-mile) radius of the town. Each one is well worth visiting for its wines, its ambience and the charm of its setting.

Kruithuis
✉ Bloem Street
☎ (021) 886 4153
📠 (021) 883 2232
🕐 09:00–15:30 Mon–Fri (Sep–May)
💰 adults R5, children 50c

Libertas Parva, Stellenryk Wine Museum and Rembrandt van Rijn Art Museum
✉ 31 Dorp Street
🕐 09:00–12:45 and 14:00–17:00 Mon–Fri, 10:00–13:00 and 14:00–17:00 Sat

Stellenbosch Wine Routes
For information on the various wine routes in the area:
☎ (021) 886 4310
📠 (021) 886 4330
✉ info@ wineroute.co.za
🖥 www. wineroute.co.za

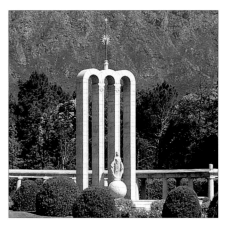

Above: *The graceful Huguenot Memorial in Franschhoek.*

<u>Franschhoek</u>
Location: Map H
Distance from Cape Town: 80km (50 miles).
Tourism Centre:
✉ 36 Market Street,
☎ (021) 876 3603,
📠 (021) 876 2768,
📧 info@
franschoek.org.za
🖥 www.
franschhoek.org.za

<u>Huguenot Memorial Museum and Monument</u>
☎ (021) 876 2673
📠 (021) 876 3649
📧 hugenoot@
museum.co.za
🖥 www.museum.co.za
🕘 09:00–17:00 Mon–Sat, 14:00–17:00 Sun

Franschhoek

The town's name – which means 'French corner' – reflects its Gallic origins: it was founded in 1688 by a party of **Huguenot** émigrés, who were refugees from a Europe torn by the religious wars. There were not a great many of them, and they were scattered among the resident Dutch and German *freeburghers* rather than allowed to form a separate community, so they soon lost their language and cultural identity. But they were hard-working and skilled folk, and they did much for the local wine industry and the architecture of the region. As a legacy of their Huguenot past, many fine estates and homesteads still bear their original French names, such as **La Provence, La Motte** and **L'Ormarins**.

The early French Huguenots and their legacy are commemorated in an imposing, though delicately graceful, **memorial**, and also in a **museum** complex in Franschhoek. The museum, a leading centre of research into Huguenot origins and culture, houses various examples of antique Cape furniture, silverware and early farm implements.

Franschhoek, set among the vineyards of the lovely valley, is part of the **Four Passes Fruit Route**. It is also a culinary mecca; its award-winning restaurants catering for a devoted clientele of national and international gourmets.

Southern Seaboard

The fast-growing town of **Somerset West** occupies the southern part of the Stellenbosch winelands, flanked by False Bay and the lofty Hottentots Holland mountains in the east. To cross these massive ramparts, you wind your way up the dizzy heights of **Sir Lowry's Pass**.

Among the attractions of the area is the **Helderberg Nature Reserve**, an expanse of heath and indigenous forest which is a sanctuary for an array of birds.

Beyond Somerset West the marine drive cuts through coastal mountains to the picturesque villages of **Gordon's Bay** and **Strand**, popular among Capetonian weekenders, upcountry holidaymakers and affluent owners of second homes. Private yachts and commercial fishing boats bob companionably together in the harbour; sunlovers make for the soft sands of Bikini and Main beaches, sporting anglers for the open sea, where fine catches of tuna and yellowtail are routinely recorded.

Further to the south are the tranquil and unspoilt holiday villages of **Pringle Bay** and **Betty's Bay**. The **Harold Porter Botanic Garden** is famed for the rich variety and beauty of its wild flowers. The town of **Kleinmond**, scenically located at the mouth of the Palmiet River, is a holiday centre with all the amenities as well as the added bonus of a relatively wind-free climate.

Somerset West
Location: Map A–D5
Distance from Cape Town: 50km
(31 miles)

Gordon's Bay
Location: Map A–D5
Distance from Cape Town: 60km
(37 miles)

Strand
Location: Map A–D5
Distance from Cape Town: 56km
(35 miles)

Betty's Bay/
Pringle Bay
Location: Map A–D6
Distance from Cape Town: 110km
(68 miles)

Kleinmond
Location: Map A–E6
Distance from Cape Town: 120km
(75 miles)

Below: *The picturesque harbour of Gordon's Bay.*

Hermanus
Location: Map A–E6
Distance from Cape
Town: 150km
(93 miles)
Tourism Centre:
✉ 36 Market Street
☎ (028) 312 2629
📠 (028) 313 0305
📧 infoburo@
hermanus.co.za
💻 www.
hermanus.co.za

Hermanus

The town, nestled between the mountains and the blue waters of **Walker Bay**, is one of the Western Cape's premier holiday spots and a magnet for whale-watchers. In the autumn and winter months these giant marine mammals, most being southern rights, come inshore. An official 'whale crier', complete with uniform and horn, announces the arrival of these leviathans.

In addition to its famous whale-watching, Hermanus offers fine beaches, safe bathing and excellent surfing. There are splendid opportunities (all along the rocky coast to either side and in the placid Kleinriviersvlei lagoon) for yachtsmen and fishermen, and also for divers in search of juicy crayfish (rock lobster) and *perlemoen* (abalone).

Highly recommended is the walk along the cliff tops, and the **Rocky Mountain Way**, a scenic drive that slices through the hills. The local 18-hole golf course welcomes visitors, as does the nearby Hamilton Russell estate, which boasts Africa's southernmost vineyards.

Among the town's more ambitious tourist schemes is its **Old Harbour**, preserved *in toto* as a museum and a national monument to the fisherfolk of yesteryear. Commercial fishermen, as well as sporting anglers and boat owners, now use the splendid new marine complex.

Below: *The Old Harbour at Hermanus, once a fishing centre and now preserved as a museum.*

Langebaan

Langebaan **lagoon**, to the north of Cape Town, is an impressive bird sanctuary. The 16km (10-mile) channel, which opens out into **Saldanha Bay**, is both one of Africa's finest wetland areas and also

the focal point of the west coast's tourism industry. Its shallow waters, the fringing mud and sand banks and the bay's islands and rocky shores, are a magnet for great concourses of summertime migrants from the Arctic and sub-Arctic regions.

The lagoon is the centrepiece of the fairly recently created **West Coast National Park**, which embraces the **Postberg Nature Reserve**; it is a haven for a variety of buck species and, in springtime, venue for a breathtaking fantasia of wild flowers. The Postberg, a 1800-ha (4448-acre) area of coastal plain and granite outcrop, offers picnic spots and 25km (16 miles) of game- and flower-viewing roads. The lagoon is much favoured by the yachting and water-sports fraternities.

Just to the north of Langebaan lagoon's entrance is **Club Mykonos**, a large, lively self-contained 'village' resort complex whose design and atmosphere owes much to the Greek Islands. Guests are housed in white-washed, Aegean- style *kaliphas*; cobbled alleys and village squares complete the picture. The excellent amenities here include several pubs, restaurants, boutiques, a well-equipped gymnasium and sports centre, and a 140-berth marina.

Above: Colonies of sea birds are a typical feature of the west coast.

Langebaan
Location: Map A–A1
Distance from Cape Town: 120km (75 miles)
Tourism Centre:
✉ Breë Street
☎ (022) 772 1515
📠 (022) 772 1531
📧 lbninfo@mweb.co.za
💻 www.langebaaninfo.com

West Coast National Park
☎ (022) 772 2144/5
📠 (022) 772 2607
💻 www.parks-sa.co.za

Club Mykonos
☎ (022) 707 7000
📠 (022) 772 2303
📧 reservations@clubmykonos.co.za
💻 www.clubmykonos.co.za

Above: *Cape Town panorama, with Table Mountain rising above the city.*

Best Times to Visit

Cape Town is a lovely place to visit at any time of the year; each month has its appeal. Perhaps the best time is from high summer through to early winter (January to May), when the wind tends to keep its peace, the sun falls ever more kindly on the face, and the suburbs and countryside begin to take on the lovely rustic colours of autumn.

Tourist Information

Cape Town is 1402km (871 miles) from Johannesburg, 1460km (907 miles) from Pretoria, and 1753km (1089 miles) from Durban. The region is well served by international and domestic airlines and by an excellent road system. Rail and passenger coach services connect the city with major centres.

Publicity Associations: Cape Town Tourism's official Visitors' Centre is in Burg Street, near the junction with Strand Street. The Centre has a comprehensive and well-organized data bank of booklets, brochures and maps covering accommodation, places of interest, eating out, shopping, special-interest routes and much else. It also produces the monthly *What's On* guide. The Centre's complex encompasses display rooms and an Internet café, wine bar, auditorium, travel clinic and art and craft shop; trained staff handle reservations for accommodation, tours, car-hire and national parks.

☎ (021) 426 4260,

📠 (021) 426 4266,

✈ info@
cape-town.org

🖥 www.
cape-town.org.

🕐 08:30–19:00 Mon–Fri, 8:30–17:00 Sat, 08:30 –12:00 Sun. The Tourism Gateway houses the regional offices of Satour (the South African Tourism Board), and information desks for the National Parks Board and the V & A Waterfront. However, it no longer takes bookings for the Table Mountain Cableway.

Entry Requirements

All visitors need passports to gain entry to South Africa. Most foreign nationals, however, are exempt from visa requirements, including citizens of the European Community, the United States, Australia, New Zealand, Japan, Austria, Brazil, Singapore, Switzerland and most southern African countries.

Health Requirements

Visitors from or passing through a yellow fever zone must be able to produce a valid International Certificate of Vaccination. Such zones extend through most of tropical Africa and South America (air travellers in airport transit are exempt from the requirements). Note that cholera and smallpox certificates are no longer needed, and there is no screening for Aids.

Getting There

By air: Cape Town international airport is 22km (14 miles) from the city, accessible from the N2 national highway. Inter-Cape operates a shuttle between the airport and central Cape Town; various car rental facilities and taxis are available at the airport – and some hotels provide courtesy transport to and from the airport.

By road: The region has an extensive and well-signposted network of national (prefix 'N'), metropolitan ('M') and regional ('R') highways. Surfaces are generally in very good condition.

Transport

Driver's licence: This must be carried at all times! Licences of neighbouring countries are valid in South Africa. So too are foreign licences provided they carry a photograph and are either printed in English or accompanied by an English-language certificate of authenticity. Alternatively, obtain an International Driving Permit before departure.

Insurance: Third Party cover is essential. Comprehensive car insurance is highly recommended. Rental firms will arrange such cover if you're hiring a car. Insurance tokens are obtainable at most points of entry for overland travellers.

Road Signs in Afrikaans

Note that, in South Africa, a traffic light is called a **robot**. Altough often expressed also in English, some common Afrikaans words you'll come across include:

Links • (left)
Regs • (right)
Stad • (city)
Straat • (street)
Weg • (road)
Rylaan • (avenue)
Lughawe • (airport)
Hawe • (harbour)
Hou oop • (keep open)
Gesluit • (closed)
Gevaar • (danger, hazard)
Verbode • (forbidden)
Ompad • (detour)
Tuin • ('garden', but often used with 'wild', e.g. *Wildtuin* – to denote a park or game reserve)
Strand • (beach)

Petrol: Cape Town, its suburbs, the outlying centres and main routes are well provided with fuel outlets and service stations. Many of them stay open 24 hours a day; others usually from around ⏰ 06:00–18:00. Petrol is sold in litres; self-service is in its infancy in South Africa; pump attendants see to fuel and service needs.

Road rules and signs: In South Africa, you drive on the left; the general **speed limit** on major routes is 120kph (75 mph), that on secondary (rural) roads is 100kph (60 mph), and in built-up areas 60kph (35 mph) unless otherwise indicated. Keep to the left, and pass on the right on highways with many lanes. Main roads are identified by colour signs and numbers rather than by name.

Maps: Excellent regional and city maps are available from the **AA, Cape Town**

Tourism and the bigger bookshops. Recommended is the *Globetrotter Travel Map of Cape Town*, and the maps in the *Globetrotter Road Atlas of South Africa* as well as the **Map Studio** series.

The Automobile Association: The AA of South Africa offers a wide range of services to members and members of affiliated motoring organizations. These include: assistance with breakdowns and other emergencies; insurance; car hire; accommodation reservations; touring, caravanning, camping advice; brochures and maps. Main regional office: ✉ AA House, ☎ toll-free number for breakdowns, emergency services and locksmith: 0800 010 101, or 0800 111 997; Mayday medical hotline, toll free 0800 033 007.

Car hire: Major, internationally known rental companies Avis,

Imperial (incorporating Hertz) and Budget maintain offices in Cape Town, at the airport and at other points throughout the wider region.

Taxis: Cape Town's cabs do not cruise the streets in search of fares (nothing like London or New York). They are found in a number of designated city ranks and at several, but by no means all, suburban railway stations. Taxi companies are listed in the Yellow Pages. If your journey involves more than a simple, cross-city hop, ask the taxi driver for an estimate of cost, and make quite sure he can locate your destination precisely.

Grab-a-Student: ☎ (021) 448 7712, 🖷 (021) 448 7714, employs students who need to earn extra money, and they drive you around in your hired car. The advantages are that they are familiar with the roads, one-ways and parking areas. They are usually a mine of information on history, tourist attractions, and often speak a foreign language. (Request your specific language preference when booking).

There are also the so-called **black taxis** – minibuses that patrol the main thoroughfares and travel to and from the townships. They are cheap, fast (sometimes too fast), sociable, often very crowded, and will stop if you hail them, but are not recommended for tourists. Rather call **Rikki Taxis**, ☎ (021) 423 4888, 🖷 (021) 423 2139; they offer a quick, three-wheeler service which covers the central area.

Buses: Regular services link the city with all major suburbs. The main bus terminal is behind (to the west of) the Golden Acre complex.

Trains: Train services connect the city with the southern, south-eastern and northeastern suburbs, but not the central and western parts of the Peninsula. The main rail terminus is on Lower Adderley Street. During the early 1990s criminals were active on some stretches of the line; security has been tightened, but rather seek advice (from Cape Town Tourism or hotel reception) before embarking on a trip beyond the nearer suburbs.

What to Pack

Cape Town can be very hot in summer, cold and damp in winter. Dress is generally informal; shorts, jeans and T-shirts are the norm in summer (beachwear, though, is appropriate only at the beach, by the pool and on private property). Sunscreen is essential. 'Smart casual' wear is often required after dark at theatres and other venues, and at the more sophisticated hotels and restaurants.

Trips and Tours by Air
For a memorable bird's-eye view of the city and surrounding areas, book a helicopter flip. Companies offer excursions ranging from a ten-minute jaunt around the city bowl and Table Mountain to an hour's flight south along the scenically stunning Atlantic seaboard to Cape Point and back over False Bay. Various tours take you farther afield – to the picturesque Winelands, for instance, where you spend time sightseeing, sampling the vintages and lunching at one of the stately homesteads. Among aerial tour operators are: Court, Sealink, Civair, Sport Helicopters and Flamingo Flights. Destinations include Hermanus, the Garden Route, Langebaan Lagoon and, in springtime, flower-bedecked Namaqualand.

Money Matters

The South African currency unit is the **Rand**, divided into 100 cents. Coins are issued in denominations of 1c, 2c, 5c, 10c, 20c, 50c, R1, R2 and R5; while notes are available in denominations of R10, R20, R50, R100 and R200.

Currency exchange: Foreign money can easily be converted into rands at banks and also through such authorized dealers as Thomas Cook and American Express.

Banks: Normal banking hours are ⏱ 09:00 to 15:30 on weekdays and 08:30 or 09:00 to 11:00 on Saturdays. There are banking and exchange facilities at Cape Town international airport. Traveller's cheques may be cashed at any bank and at many hotels and shops.

Credit cards: Most hotels, restaurants, shops, car rental companies and tour operators accept international credit cards (American Express, Bank of America, Visa, Diners Club, Mastercard). Note that you cannot buy petrol with a credit card; most banks issue special 'Petrocards'.

Value Added Tax (VAT): A 14% Value Added Tax is levied on all sales of goods and services. This is usually reflected in the quoted price. Foreign visitors can claim back VAT paid on items that are to be taken out of the country (retain the tax invoice for this purpose).

Tipping: Provided you receive satisfactory service, it is usual to tip porters, waiters and waitresses, taxi drivers, room attendants, golf caddies and petrol attendant. Gratuities for providers of quantifiable services (such as waiters and taxi drivers) should amount to at least 10% of the cost of the service; for non-

quantifiable services of a minor nature (porterage, for example), it is customary to proffer about R5.
Service charges: Hotels may not by law levy a charge for general services (though there is often a telephone service loading). Restaurants may levy such a charge; few do so.

Business Hours

Normal trading and business hours are ☺ Mon–Fri 08:30–17:00, Sat 08:30–13:00. Most supermarkets stay open till 18:00, later on Fridays, and on Saturday afternoons and Sunday mornings. Corner cafés and sub-urban mini-markets stay open from early to late every day of the week. Liquor stores close at 18:30. V & A Waterfront shops (Victoria Wharf) offer night shopping.

Time Difference

Throughout the year, South African Standard Time is two hours ahead of Greenwich Mean (or Universal Standard) Time, one hour ahead of European Winter Time, and seven hours ahead of United States Eastern Standard Winter Time.

Communications

The telephone system is fully automatic; and one can dial direct to most parts of the world. The telephone directory lists dialling codes. Both local and long-distance calls are metred. Dial 1023 for directory queries. Fax transmission facilities are widely available. Public call boxes accept either coins or Telkom phone cards.

Most post offices are open from ☺ 08:00 to 16:30 weekdays and 08:00 to 12:00 noon Sat. An international priority mail service is available. Stamps are available at CNA and some cafés and supermarkets. The major English-language dailies are

Man of Destiny
Nelson Mandela, South African president from 1994–99, was incarcerated for treason on Robben Island. Born in 1918 into the royal Tembu (Xhosa) house in the Transkei region of the Eastern Cape, Mandela qualified as a lawyer during the 1940s and quickly became prominent in the movement to liberate the country from apartheid, helping found Umkhonto we Sizwe, the military wing of the African National Congress, in the 1950s. Finally indicted for conspiring to commit nearly 200 acts of sabotage he was convicted at the famed Rivonia trial of 1963 and sentenced to life imprisonment. On his release in 1990 he chose the path of peace, employing his skills and immense moral stature to lead South Africa to freedom and democracy.

the *Cape Times*, *Business Day* (morning) and *The Cape Argus* (afternoon). The latter brings out special Saturday and Sunday editions. Also available are the national weekly newspapers *The Mail and Guardian*, *The Sunday Times* and *The Sunday Independent*, and Afrikaans papers. Foreign newspapers are sold by selected news-agents and in some hotels.

Embassies and Consulates

Most countries have diplomatic representation in South Africa, maintaining their principal offices in Pretoria. They are listed in the Yellow Pages (under Consulates and Embassies) and in telephone directories (listed under the country's name).

Electricity

220/230 volts AC at 50 cycles/second; 15-amp 3-pronged (round pin) plugs. Most hotel rooms have 110 volt outlets. Not all electric shavers will fit hotel plug points; visitors should seek advice about adaptors from a local electrical supplier.

Weights and Measures

South Africa uses the metric system.

Medical Matters

Visitors are responsible for their own arrangements, and are urged to take out medical insurance before departure. Private doctors are listed in the telephone directory under 'Medical Practitioners'. Hospitalization is usually arranged through a medical practitioner, but in an emergency a visitor may telephone or go directly to the casualty department of a General (public) Hospital (listed under 'H' in the telephone directory).

Public hospitals tend to be very crowded and the staff are invariably overworked (although they do manage to maintain surprisingly high standards of treatment and care). Private hospitals generally offer more comfort and individual attention, but are a lot more expensive.

Aids: The incidence of HIV infection and AIDS-related diseases has increased dramatically over the past number of years and threatens to reach critical proportions. The South African authorities were originally slow to recognize the extent of the crisis, and also slow to act, but they eventually launched a credible publicity and prevention programme. The risk of contracting HIV, though, is no greater in South Africa than in any other country, provided the standard precautions are taken.

Safety and Security

Do not walk through the streets alone at night; avoid deserted and poorer areas unless you're with a conducted group. Don't carry large sums of cash around with you; don't leave any valuables in your room (use the hotel's security box).

Emergency Numbers

Police emergency response unit (Flying Squad): ☎ 10111; Metro: ☎ (021) 943 378; Ambulance: ☎ 10177 or 1022; Fire Brigade: ☎ (021) 535 1100; Mountain Rescue: ☎ 10177 or 10111; Sea Rescue: ☎ (021) 449 3500; Aviation Emergency: ☎ (021) 937 1116/7; Poison Information Centres: Red Cross Children's Hospital, Rondebosch, ☎ (021) 689 5227, or Tygerberg Hospital, Bellville, ☎ (021) 938 4911;

Police HQ, Caledon Square: ☎ (021) 467 8077; Police (Tourist Assistance Unit): ☎ (021) 418 2853; Chris Barnard Memorial Hospital: ☎ (021) 480 6111; National Enquiries: ☎ 10212; Cell (mobile) phone general emergencies: ☎ 112.

Photography

Most international film brands and sizes are readily available in Cape Town's photographic shops and department stores; processing is quick (same-day; one-hour at some outlets).

Language

South Africa has no fewer than 11 official languages; those most commonly spoken in and around Cape Town are English, Afrikaans (the home language of most of the Coloured people) and Xhosa (the home language of most of the Cape's black residents).

INDEX OF SIGHTS

GENERAL INDEX

GENERAL INDEX